D

D0927877

House Wiring Simplified

Based on the 2005 NEC®

Floyd M. Mix

Publisher
The Goodheart-Willcox Company Inc.
Tinley Park, Illinois

Library of Congress Catalog Card Number 2004059905
International Standard Book Number 1-59070-437-1

1 2 3 4 5 6 7 8 9 – 05 – 09 08 07 06 05

The Goodheart-Willcox Company, Inc. Brand Disclaimer: Brand names, company names, and illustrations for products and services included in this text are provided for educational purposes only and do not represent or imply endorsement or recommendation by the author or the publisher.

The Goodheart-Willcox Company, Inc. Safety Notice: The reader is expressly advised to carefully read, understand, and apply all safety precautions and warnings described in this book or that might also be indicated in undertaking the activities and exercises described herein to minimize risk of personal injury or injury to others. Common sense and good judgment should also be exercised and applied to help avoid all potential hazards. The reader should always refer to the appropriate manufacturer's technical information, directions, and recommendations; then proceed with care to follow specific equipment operating instructions. The reader should understand these notices and cautions are not exhaustive.

The publisher makes no warranty or representation whatsoever, either expressed or implied, including but not limited to equipment, procedures, and applications described or referred to herein, their quality, performance, merchantability, or fitness for a particular purpose. The publisher assumes no responsibility for any changes, errors, or omissions in this book. The publisher specifically disclaims any liability whatsoever, including any direct, indirect, incidental, consequential, special, or exemplary damages resulting, in whole or in part, from the reader's use or reliance upon the information, instructions, procedures, warnings, cautions, applications or other matter contained in this book. The publisher assumes no responsibility for the activities of the reader.

(This printing is updated to the 2005 National Electrical Code.)

Library of Congress Cataloging-in-Publication Data

Mix, Floyd M.
    House wiring simplified: based on the 2005 NEC
Floyd M. Mix.
        p. cm.
    Includes index.
    ISBN 1-59070-437-1
        1. Electric wiring, Interior—Amateurs' manuals.
    2. Dwellings—Maintenance and repair—Amateurs'
manuals   I. Title

TK3285.M57 2005
621.319'24—dc22   2004059905
                                                  CIP

Introduction

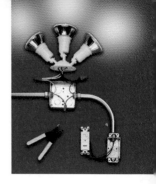

House Wiring Simplified teaches the fundamentals of basic, safe house wiring procedures.

It shows, in easy-to-understand drawings, how to install wiring that will serve *safely* and *effectively*, the lighting, appliance, and equipment needs of today, as well as tomorrow. It covers both new homes and older homes.

House Wiring Simplified tells how to determine what wiring is needed, what equipment and what materials to use. Because *National Electrical Code* requirements vary, users are cautioned to check local codes. For example, this text shows installation of EMT (thinwall conduit) in its installation illustrations. Local variation may allow use of armored cable (BX) or nonmetallic flexible cable.

Review questions have been included in this book for these reasons:

❏ They will help you determine which material you have learned and which material you should restudy.

❏ They summarize for you many important items with which you should become familiar.

You can see if your answers are correct, by referring to the answers in the back of the book. Be fair with yourself. Answer the questions (on a separate sheet of paper) before you refer to the correct answers.

House Wiring Simplified is intended for students in high school, vocational school, college, apprentice training, and adult classes. It will also enable the homeowner to handle many residential wiring jobs he or she was reluctant to tackle before.

Floyd M. Mix

Contents

Safety Rules

Only by learning and faithfully following certain safety rules can the electrician hope to avoid accidents and injury. The basic rules are:

1. Remain alert. **Think** before acting.
2. Avoid quick movements. Work carefully and deliberately. Plan each step of your work.
3. Avoid live work unless absolutely necessary. Disconnect circuit at its main source, if possible.
4. Make certain a circuit is de-energized. Test it with a test light before beginning work on it.
5. Use tools correctly and for their intended purpose. Use only tools with insulated handles when working on live circuits. Keep tools in good working order.
6. Remove jewelry, rings, watches, and other metal objects or apparel from the body before beginning work.
7. Make sure all electrical equipment is properly grounded.
8. Keep work areas dry and free of debris. If necessary, clear the area of loose material or hanging objects. Cover wet floors with wooden planking. Wear rubber boots or rubber soled shoes.
9. Wear gloves when possible.
10. Place a rubber barrier or other nonconductive shield around exposed conductors or equipment near the work area.
11. Lift objects carefully. Use the leg muscles. Keep back straight while lifting.
12. Wear clothing that is neither floppy nor too tight. Loose clothing will catch on corners and rough surfaces causing unsafe motion. Clothing that binds is uncomfortable and may be just as unsafe as clothing that is too loose.
13. Wear safety glasses when using striking tools.

Unit 1
Electrical Terms

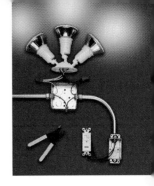

In house wiring, we make frequent reference to the terms *volts, amperes, watts.*

It is easy to understand these terms if we compare the flow of electricity through a wire to the flow of water through a pipe. See **Figure 1-1.**

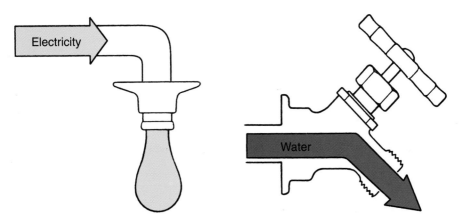

Figure 1-1. Electricity flows through wire much like the way water flows through pipe.

Voltage

Water pressure in a pipe can be compared to electrical pressure in a conductor. Water pressure is measured by pounds per square inch. Electric pressure, or *voltage,* is measured in *volts (V).*

Current

In measuring the amount of water passing through a pipe, the term gallons is used. In electricity, the number of electrons flowing, the *current,* is measured. The unit of measurement for current is *amperes (A).* Various parts of a wiring system—circuit breakers, switches, receptacles, etc.—are rated in amperes. The rating of the components in amperes indicates the greatest amount of current with which they should be used.

Resistance

Resistance can be described as electrical friction or the tendency of a conductor (wire) to keep the electric current from passing through it. Electrical energy lost is given off as heat. Conductors such as copper, silver, and aluminum, offer very little resistance to the flow of electric current. Examples of poor conductors (insulators) are glass, wood, and paper. The unit measure of resistance is the *ohm* (Ω). We speak of ohms of resistance in electricity like we speak of pounds of pull required to break a certain fishing line.

Ohm's Law

Using a formula known as *Ohm's law,* voltage, current, or resistance can be calculated if the other two factors are known. The formulas for Ohm's law are as follows:

$$\text{Voltage} = \text{Current} \times \text{Resistance}$$
$$\text{Current} = \text{Voltage} \div \text{Resistance}$$
$$\text{Resistance} = \text{Voltage} \div \text{Current}$$

Power

The *watt (W)* is the unit of measurement *power.* It tells us how much electricity is being used. Watts consumed are determined by using the following formula.

$$\text{Power} = \text{Voltage} \times \text{Current}$$
or
$$\text{Watts} = \text{Volts} \times \text{Amperes}$$

One *kilowatt* is equal to 1000 watts. One *kilowatt hour (kWh)* is equal to 1000 watts used for one hour. The *kilowatt hour* is the unit by which electricity is metered (sold).

Circuit

In an *electrical circuit,* a wire or path is provided for electricity to flow from the power source (such as a generator or distribution box) to the final use (such as an electric light or appliance) and back. See **Figure 1-2.**

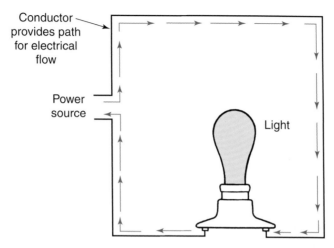

Conductor provides path for electrical flow

Power source

Light

Figure 1-2. A simple electrical circuit. Arrows show the electrical path.

Switch

A *switch* is a device for controlling the flow of current in an electric circuit by opening and closing the circuit, **Figure 1-3.** With the switch in the open position, there is no electrical connection between the terminals.

Figure 1-3. Knife type switch (for low voltage only) in open position. The open circuit means that no electricity will flow.

Direct Current

Direct current (dc) flows only in one direction. Batteries (such as storage and dry cell) are important sources of direct current. One terminal of a battery is always positive (+) and the other is always negative (–).

Alternating Current

In *alternating current (ac)*, the voltage flows first in one direction, then the other. Each two reversals of the direction of the current is called a cycle. The number of cycles per second is called the *frequency*. The unit measure of frequency is *hertz (Hz)*. There is a very short interval of time between changes of direction when no current is flowing.

Most house wiring in the United States is 60 cycle (or 60 hertz). You may wonder why an electric light operated by current which changes direction of flow 60 times per second does not flicker. This is because the filament in the lightbulb does not have time to cool while there is no current flowing.

Review Questions

Please do not write in the text. Place your answers on a separate sheet of paper.

Matching quiz. Match the terms in the column at the left with the proper definition on the right:

a. Alternating current.
b. Amperes.
c. Direct current.
d. Kilowatt hour.
e. Ohms.
f. Resistance.
g. Switch.
h. Volts.
i. Watts.

1. _____ Unit of measurement of electrical pressure.
2. _____ Unit of measurement of electrical current.
3. _____ Unit of measurement of how much electricity a device uses.
4. _____ Unit by which electricity is metered.
5. _____ Unit of measurement of electrical resistance.
6. _____ Tendency of conductor to keep electric current from passing through it.
7. _____ Device for controlling current by opening or closing circuit.
8. _____ Current flowing in one direction only.
9. _____ Current flowing first in one direction, then in the other.

Unit 2
Conductors

In house wiring, electrical conductors provide paths for the flow of electric current. These paths are wires over which an insulating material is formed. Insulation is a noncurrent-carrying material that ensures the current flow will be through the wire.

Wire Size and Color

The drawing, **Figure 2-1,** shows the actual size of conductors, without insulation. Note that as the numbers become larger, the size of the wire decreases. For most house wiring jobs, copper wire numbers 12 and 14 are specified by the building plans. Numbers 6 and 8 wires, which are available either as solid wire or stranded wire, are used for heavy power circuits, and as service entrance leads into buildings.

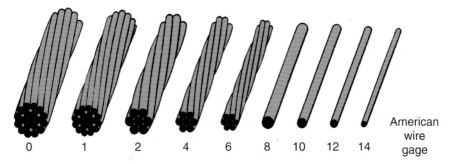

Figure 2-1. Copper conductor sizes are listed by gage number. The wire gets smaller as the gage numbers get larger.

Figure 2-2 shows the current-carrying capacities of conductors of various sizes. In house wiring, considerable use is made of single wire conductors, **Figure 2-3.**

For many installations, the use of individual wires spaced and supported side-by-side would be inefficient and impractical. Instead, conductor cables consisting of insulated wires arranged in pairs or groups of three or more are used. The manufacturer forms or winds additional insulating or protective material around the insulated wires.

11

In a 2-wire cable, one wire is black and one wire is white. In a 3-wire cable the extra wire is red. The white wire is a neutral wire. The colored wires, with the exception of green wires, are "hot" wires. The green, or ground, wire will be discussed later. Under certain conditions, grounding wires may be bare and uninsulated.

PROPERTIES OF COPPER CONDUCTORS				
			Resistance	
Size (AWG)	Diameter (in.)	Area (in.²)	Uncoated (Ω/1000 ft.)	Coated (Ω/1000 ft.)
18	0.040	0.001	7.77	8.08
16	0.051	0.002	4.89	5.08
14	0.064	0.003	3.07	3.19
12	0.081	0.005	1.93	2.01
10	0.102	0.008	1.21	1.26
8	0.128	0.013	0.764	0.786
6	0.184	0.027	0.491	0.510
4	0.232	0.042	0.308	0.321
3	0.260	0.053	0.245	0.254
2	0.292	0.067	0.194	0.201
1	0.332	0.087	0.154	0.160
1/0	0.372	0.109	0.122	0.127
2/0	0.418	0.137	0.0967	0.101
3/0	0.470	0.173	0.0766	0.0797
4/0	0.528	0.219	0.0608	0.0626

Figure 2-2. Properties of copper conductors. Properties for sizes up to No. 8 are for single conductors. No. 6 and larger are stranded conductors.

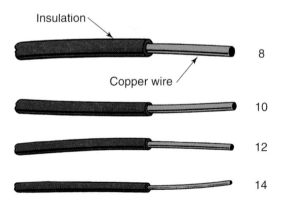

Figure 2-3. Single wire conductors.

Nonmetallic and Armored Cable

In modern house wiring, two types of cable are commonly used: nonmetallic sheathed cable and flexible armored cable. *Nonmetallic sheathed cable* is an assembly of two or more insulated wires with an outer sheath or covering of moisture-resistant, nonmetallic material. Examine **Figures 2-4** and **2-5**. *Flexible armored cable*, commonly referred to as BX, comes in 2- and 3-wire types, **Figure 2-6**. Armored cable has wires with insulation and a bare ground wire twisted

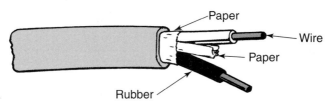

Figure 2-4. Two-wire nonmetallic sheathed cable without ground.

Figure 2-5. Two-wire sheathed cable with ground wire.

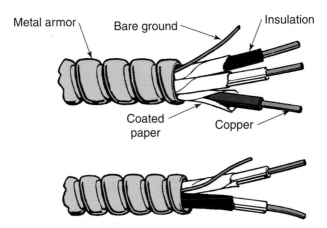

Figure 2-6. Metallic armored cable. Top—Three-wire cable with bare ground. Bottom—Two-wire cable with bare ground.

together. This grouping of wires is then wrapped in coated paper and covered with self-locking steel armor. Several types of insulation are listed in **Figure 2-7**.

Wire and Cable Insulations	
Type and insulation	Letter type
Thermoplastic:	
Thermoplastic and Fibrous Outer Braid	TBS
Flame Retardant Heat Resistant	THHN
Flame Retardant Moisture and Heat Resistant	THHW
Flame Retardant Moisture and Heat Resistant	THW
Flame Retardant Moisture and Heat Resistant	THWN
Flame Retardant Moisture Resistant	TW
Underground Feeder and Branch Circuit Moisture Resistant	UF
Underground Service Entrance Heat and Moisture Resistant	USE
Thermoset:	
Thermoset	RHH
Flame Retardant Moisture Resistant Thermoset	RHW
Flame Retardant Thermoset	XHH
Flame Retardant Moisture Resistant Thermoset	XHHW
Other polymer types:	
Perflouro-alkoxy	PFA
Silicone rubber	SA
Extended polytetra-flouro-ethylene	TFE
Modified Ethylene tetrafluoro-ethylene	Z
Modified Ethylene tetrafluoro-ethylene	ZW

Figure 2-7. Types of wire and cable insulation. The letter designations are those of the National Electrical Code.

Cords

Flexible electric cords are commonly grouped and designated as lamp, heater, and power or service cords.

Lamp cords

Lamp cords, also called fixture cords, are flexible cords that are used to connect lamps, radios, etc., to outlets. Lamp cord is made up of fine strands to give it flexibility. It is then covered with thermoplastic insulation. Lamp and fixture cords are designated as SPT 16/2 and SPT 18/2. See **Figures 2-8** and **2-9.**

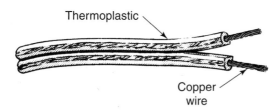

Thermoplastic

Copper
wire

Figure 2-8. (SPT 16/2) Plastic covered flexible lamp cord.

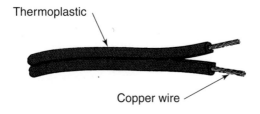

Thermoplastic

Copper wire

Figure 2-9. This lamp cord, lighter than the cord in Figure 2-8, is designated as SPT 18/.2.

Heater cords

For heating appliances such as electric irons, toasters, and waffle irons, a special cord called a **heater cord** is used. This has a layer of paper-wrapped nylon around each rubber-covered wire, and an overall covering of plastic or rubber, **Figure 2-10.**

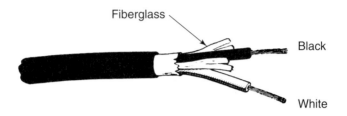

Figure 2-10. Type SJ cord is used for appliances and heaters.

Power or service cords

Electric cords used for large motors, heavy-duty power tools, and devices with similar power requirements must be heavy enough to carry the load without overheating. See **Figure 2-11.** These types of cords are called *power* or *service cords.*

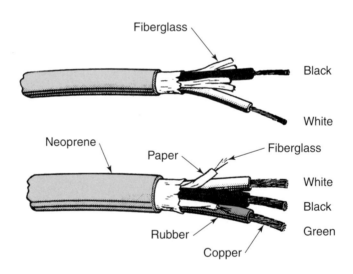

Figure 2-11. Power or service cord. Top—Two-wire cord. Botom—Three-wire cord.

Other cord types available

Figure 2-12 illustrates some special-purpose cords. As you progress with your house wiring activities, you will find that many other types of conductors are available.

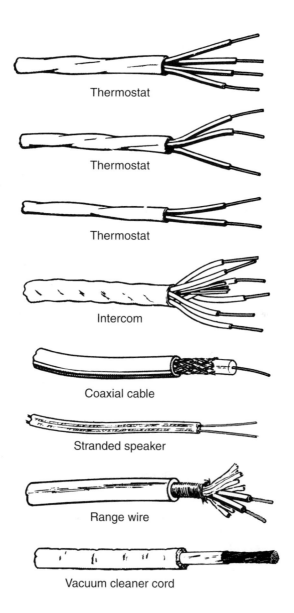

Thermostat

Thermostat

Thermostat

Intercom

Coaxial cable

Stranded speaker

Range wire

Vacuum cleaner cord

Figure 2-12. Special purpose cords.

Wiring Must Meet Codes

All house wiring must be installed in accordance with city and state codes or regulations applicable to the work being done. The wiring must also comply with the *National Electrical Code*®. Requirements of the local utility company must also be met.

Compliance with codes usually results in installations free from electrical hazards. However, the systems will not necessarily be efficient, convenient, or adequate for good service and future expansion.

Electrical codes are *not* intended as construction guides for untrained people.

The **National Electrical Code (NEC),** which contains rules and specifications intended to safeguard both people and property from hazards arising from the use of electricity, is sponsored by the:

National Fire Protection Association, Inc.
1 Batterymarch Park,
Quincy, MA 02169-7471.

A copy of the *Code* is an important tool for everyone interested in house wiring procedures.

Using approved materials and devices

When installing house wiring, only Underwriters Laboratories (UL) approved materials and devices should be used. Underwriters Laboratories, which is supported by manufacturers, insurance companies, and other interested parties, tests materials and devices to see if they meet certain minimum electrical standards.

The Underwriters' label (several styles used), which is stamped on or printed and attached to items that have been approved, assures the purchaser that minimum safety requirements as specified by the National Electrical Code have been met. However, the approval stamp is not intended to convey the idea that all approved items are of equal quality.

Careful installation

All wiring and fixtures should be installed in a neat, exacting manner. Closely follow all the plans (working drawings) provided for the job.

Review Questions

Please do not write in the text. Place your answers on a separate sheet of paper.

1. Insulation is a (noncurrent/current) carrying material that ensures the current will flow through the wire.
2. As the size of the wire decreases, the wire number becomes (larger/smaller).
3. For most house wiring jobs, copper wire numbers _____ and _____ are specified by the building plans.
4. In a 2-wire cable, the wire colors are: _____ and _____.
5. In a 3-wire cable, the wire colors are: _____, _____, and _____.
6. *True or False?* The neutral wire is always white.
7. List the two types of cables commonly used in modern house wiring.
   a. _____
   b. _____
8. Flexible electric cords are grouped under the following three headings.
   a. _____
   b. _____
   c. _____
9. All house wiring must be installed according to:
   a. City and state codes.
   b. National Electrical Code.
   c. Local utility company requirements.
   d. All of the above.
   e. None of the above.
10. Only _____ _____ approved materials and devices should be used when doing house wiring.

Student electricians installing electrical wiring systems at a national SkillsUSA contest. They will be judged on competence and knowledge of electrical code requirements, as well as their skills.

Unit 3
Conduits and Raceways

Conduit is a type of tubing (metal or plastic) that is used to enclose and protect electrical wiring.

Rigid Steel Conduit

Rigid steel conduit is available both in galvanized and black enameled types. This conduit comes in 10 ft. lengths. Both ends of the conduit are threaded and a coupling is screwed on one end, **Figure 3-1.** Sizes range from 1/2 to 6 in., **Figure 3-2.** Rigid conduit, which is bendable, is cut and threaded with the same type of tools as used for water pipe.

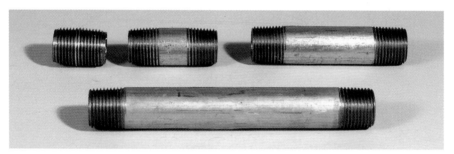

Figure 3-1. Rigid steel conduit and nipples.

Thinwall Steel Conduit

Thinwall conduit, which is the type of conduit used for most house wiring, is galvanized, light in weight, and is easy to bend and handle. It comes in 10 ft. lengths, without couplings. The wall is so thin it cannot be threaded. Special pressure fittings are used to couple joints together and to connect the conduit to switch and outlet boxes. See **Figures 3-3, 3-4,** and **3-5.**

Size (in inches)	Diameter (inches) External	Internal	Thickness (in inches)
1/2	0.840	0.622	0.109
3/4	1.050	0.824	0.113
1	1.315	1.049	0.133
1 1/4	1.660	1.380	0.140
1 1/2	1.900	1.610	0.145
2	2.375	2.067	0.154
2 1/2	2.875	2.469	0.203
3	3.500	3.068	0.216
3 1/2	4.000	3.548	0.226
4	4.500	4.026	0.237
5	5.563	5.047	0.258
6	6.625	6.065	0.280

Figure 3-2. Chart for rigid conduit showing thickness and internal and external diameters.

Figure 3-3. Thinwall conduit.

Figure 3-4. Typical thinwall fittings.

Aluminum Rigid Conduit

Aluminum rigid conduit comes in 10 ft. lengths. It usually comes threaded on both ends. One end is fitted with a coupling. The other end is fitted with a plastic protector to protect the threads. See **Figures 3-6** and **3-7**.

Trade size (inches)	Outside diameter (inches)	Nominal inside diameter (inches)	Nominal wall thickness (inches)	Nominal weight per 100 ft. (pounds)
3/8	0.577	0.493	0.042	23
1/2	0.706	0.622	0.042	30
3/4	0.922	0.824	0.049	47
1	1.163	1.049	0.057	68
1 1/4	1.510	1.380	0.065	100
1 1/2	1.740	1.610	0.065	114
2	2.197	2.067	0.065	147
2 1/2	2.875	2.731	0.072	230
3	3.500	3.356	0.072	270
4	4.500	4.334	0.083	400

Figure 3-5. Chart for thinwall conduit showing dimensions and weight.

Figure 3-6. Aluminum rigid conduit.

Size (in inches)	O.D. (in inches)	I.D. (in inches)	Wall Thickness (in inches)	Weight per Length
1/2	0.840	0.622	0.109	3.0
3/4	1.050	0.824	0.113	4.0
1	1.315	1.049	0.133	6.0
1 1/4	1.660	1.380	0.140	8.1
1 1/2	1.900	1.610	0.145	9.7
2	2.375	2.067	0.154	13.2
2 1/2	2.875	2.469	0.203	20.8
3	3.500	3.068	0.216	27.2
3 1/2	4.000	3.548	0.226	32.7
4	4.500	4.026	0.237	38.9
5	5.563	5.047	0.258	52.9
6	6.625	6.065	0.280	78.7

Figure 3-7. Chart for aluminum rigid conduit showing diameter, wall thickness, and weight.

Flexible Steel Conduit

Flexible steel conduit, commonly called *greenfield*, is similar in construction to BX. However, greenfield contains no wires.

Greenfield is sometimes used with rigid conduit where the runs involve short, difficult bends. Wires are pulled through the greenfield after installation. See **Figures 3-8** and **3-9.**

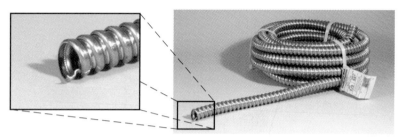

Figure 3-8. Flexible steel conduit without wires is frequently called greenfield.

Size (in inches)	Feet in coil	Wt. lbs. per 100 ft.	Size (in inches)	Feet in coil	Wt. lbs. per 100 ft.
5/16	250	15	1 1/4	50	125
3/8	250	25	1 1/2	25	162
1/2	100	47	2	25	213
3/4	50	58	2 1/2	25	263
1	50	102	3	25	313

Figure 3-9. Chart showing greenfield sizes and weights.

Rigid Plastic Conduit

Conduit made from polyvinyl chloride compound (PVC) has established its ability to retain outstanding properties. It will withstand immersion in water or oil and exposure to sunlight, underground moisture, and corrosive atmospheres. PVC conduit comes in 1/2 to 4 in. diameters and in 10 and 20 ft. lengths. PVC can come with plain or threaded ends.

Surface Raceways

Metal *raceways,* **Figure 3-10,** are installed on the surface. They provide mechanical protection to conductors while keeping them accessible for wiring changes. On rewiring jobs, the surface installation of raceways eliminates dealing with in-wall wiring. The raceways can be finished to match the surrounding surfaces.

Metal raceways should be selected on the basis of the number and size of conductors to be carried. Always use specifications and instructions supplied by the manufacturer. Many different systems are available. These include raceways in which wires are pulled through, prewired systems, plug-in strips, and overfloor systems. See **Figure 3-11** for examples of overfloor systems.

Raceways can be mounted on almost any type of surface using the fastening methods shown in **Figure 3-12.**

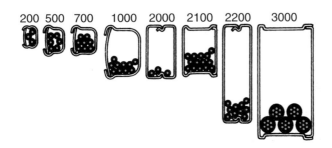

Figure 3-10. Surface mounted metal raceways. (Wiremold Co.)

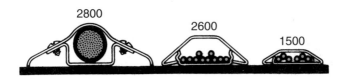

Figure 3-11. Overfloor type of surface mounted metal raceways.

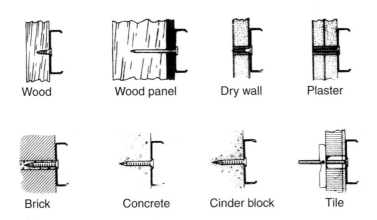

Figure 3-12. Ways to mount metal raceways.

Review Questions

Please do not write in the text. Place your answers on a separate sheet of paper.

1. Metal or plastic tubing used to enclose or protect electrical wiring is called _____.
2. Rigid conduit is cut and threaded with the same tools as used for _____.
3. Thinwall steel conduit uses special _____ to couple joints and to connect to switch and outlet boxes.
4. Rigid plastic conduit will withstand immersion in _____ or _____.
5. Flexible steel conduit is similar in construction to _____, but it contains no wires.
6. On rewiring jobs, raceway surface installation eliminates dealing with _____ wiring.
7. Metal raceways should be selected on the basis of the _____ and _____ of conductors to be carried.

Unit 4
Boxes and Covers

In modern house wiring, all conductor joints or connections must be housed in approved electrical boxes, and the boxes must be mounted where they will be accessible for making wiring changes. All switches and outlets must also be housed in boxes, and all fixtures must be mounted on boxes.

Box Construction

Both steel and nonmetallic (plastic) boxes are available. The metal boxes are made of heavy galvanized steel, usually 14 gage, and come in four principal shapes: square, octagon, rectangular, and circular. See **Figures 4-1** to **4-6** inclusive.

Outlet boxes made from steel have knockouts. *Knockouts* are machine punched pieces of metal not completely cut loose from the metal box. They are removed to insert conduit and cable. See **Figure 4-7**. The knockout with the slot, shown at the left in Figure 4-7, is removed by inserting a screwdriver and prying.

Figure 4-1. Left—Octagon-shaped junction or ceiling outlet box. Right—Outlet box extension.

Figure 4-2. Rectangular-shaped switch or outlet box with square corners.

Figure 4-3. Rectangular-shaped switch or outlet box with beveled corners and clamps for connecting cable.

Figure 4-4. Round, shallow ceiling box. Boxes of this kind are used mostly on "old work" rewiring jobs.

Figure 4-5. Surface mounted box.

Disk-shaped knockouts can be easily removed. Use a punch or heavy screwdriver to bend the disk outward, and use a pair of pliers to break it off.

Box Covers or Plates

Boxes used for house wiring connections, switches, and outlets must be covered. Usually when a fixture is mounted on the box, no other cover is required.

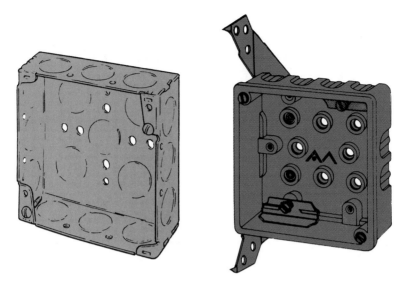

Figure 4-6. Left—Square metal junction box. Right—Square plastic junction box.

Figure 4-7. Left—Two types of box knockouts. Right—Knockout seal.

Figure 4-8 shows an assortment of single, duplex, and gang type plates. A variety of telephone plates are shown in **Figure 4-9.** Most wiring jobs can be completed using one or more of the plates shown. Plates for many specialized purposes are also available.

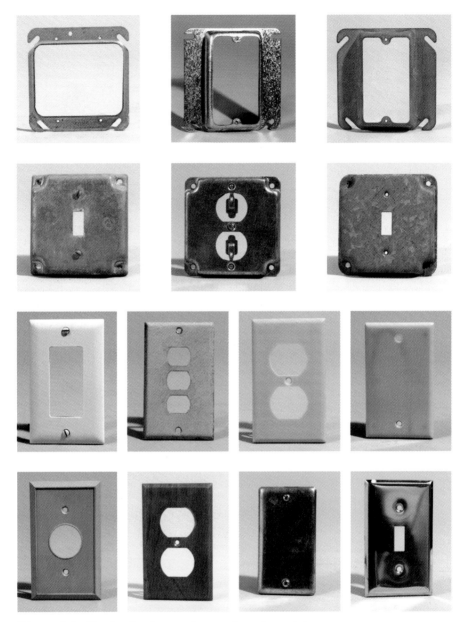

Figure 4-8. Single, duplex, and gang type box plates or covers.

Figure 4-8. (Continued) Additional box plates or covers.

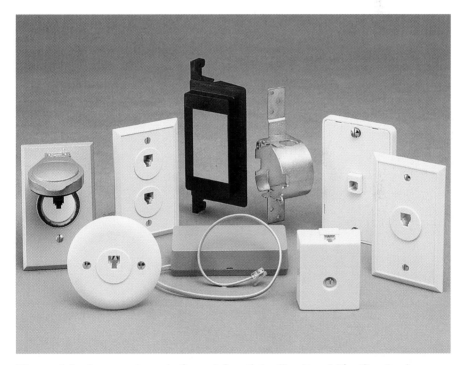

Figure 4-9. An assortment of special outlets. (Leviton Mfg. Co., Inc.)

Review Questions

Please do not write in the text. Place your answers on a separate sheet of paper.

1. *True or False?* Boxes must house all conductor joints or connections.
2. *True or False?* Boxes should be mounted so they will be accessible for making wiring changes.
3. *True or False?* Boxes must house all switches and outlets.
4. *True or False?* Boxes must be used to mount all fixtures.
5. List the four basic shapes of metal boxes.
    a. _____
    b. _____
    c. _____
    d. _____
6. Punched pieces of metal not completely cut loose from the box that are removed to insert conduit and cable are called _____.
7. Usually a cover is not required on a box used for:
    a. wiring connections.
    b. switches.
    c. outlets.
    d. fixtures.

Unit 5
Switches

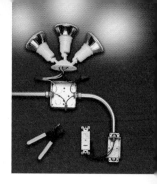

Single-Pole Switches

The *single-pole switch,* **Figure 5-1,** has two terminals. This switch turns one light or appliance on and off from a single location. **Figure 5-2** shows how a typical single-pole switch works. A different (more quiet) type of single-pole switch is illustrated in **Figures 5-3** and **5-4.**

Figure 5-5 shows a mercury-operated switch that is completely silent. Electrical contact in this switch is made by mercury moving within a hermetically (airtight) sealed button. There are no mechanical parts to snap or click.

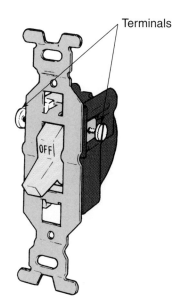

Figure 5-1. Single-pole switch.

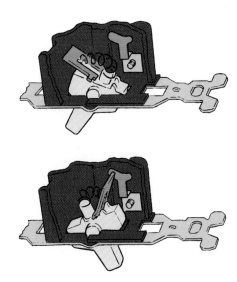

Figure 5-2. Top—Single-pole switch in the *off* position. Bottom—Same switch in the *on* position.

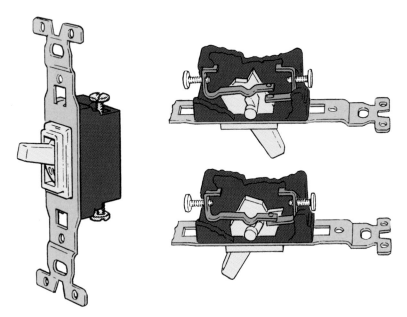

Figure 5-3. Single-pole switch of the quiet type.

Figure 5-4. How the quiet-type switch, shown in Figure 5-3, works.

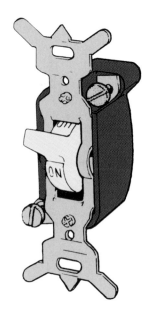

Figure 5-5. Single-pole mercury operated switch that is completely silent in operation.

A delayed-action switch is shown in **Figure 5-6.** With a delayed-action switch you turn the switch off, but the device does not immediately shut off. When used with a lighting system, you can turn the switch off and, as you walk away, the lights stay on 30 to 60 seconds before shutting off.

Figure 5-7 shows a single-pole touch switch. The button is pushed to turn the light on and off.

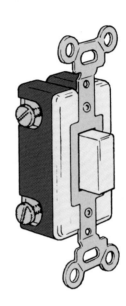

Figure 5-6. Delayed-action switch.   **Figure 5-7.** Single-pole touch switch.

Canopy switches—tumbler, pull chain, and push-button, **Figure 5-8**—are small size, compact switches mounted in the canopies of lighting fixtures, to control the lamps at the fixtures.

A feed through switch inserted in a portable cord is shown in **Figure 5-9.**

Three-Way Switches

Three-way switches, **Figure 5-10,** are used to control lights from two locations. Note the three terminals. Two 3-way switches are required for each installation. **Figure 5-11** shows how a 3-way switch works. See Figures 12-9, 12-10, and 12-11 for 3-way switch wiring diagrams.

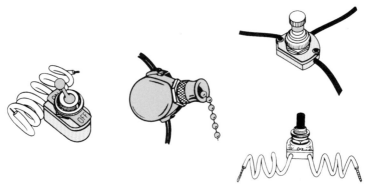

Figure 5-8. Small canopy switches. Left—Tumbler. Center—Pull chain. Right—Push-button.

Figure 5-9. Feed through switch used in portable cord.

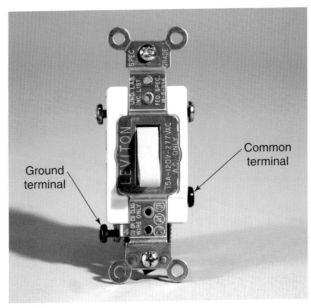

Figure 5-10. Three-way switch. Note the three terminals.

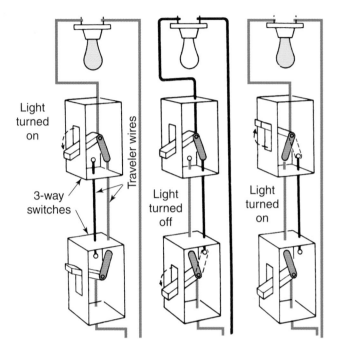

Figure 5-11. How a 3-way switch works. The circuit is completed by moving either switch up or down.

Four-Way Switches

Four-way switches (each switch has four terminals), **Figure 5-12,** are used when we want to control an electrical circuit from three points. When using a 4-way switch, it is necessary to use two 3-way switches in the circuit. One 4-way switch is installed between the two 3-way switches. **Figure 5-13** shows how a 4-way switch works. For an installation diagram, see Figure 12-12.

For each additional control point, an additional 4-way switch must be inserted between the two 3-way switches.

Dimmer Switch

The *dimmer switch* is used to switch a light from bright light (100%) to dim light (about 25%). The switch is controlled by a sliding knob, as shown in **Figure 5-14,** or a rotating knob. Installation is done by replacing the regular switch with a dimmer switch.

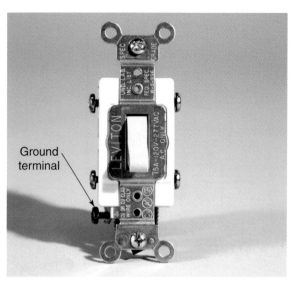

Figure 5-12. Four-way switch. Note the four current-carrying terminals.

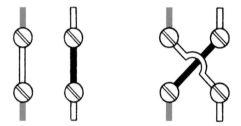

Figure 5-13. A 4-way switch is a special double pole, double-throw switch, used between two 3-way switches to provide an additional switch from which a light can be operated. When the switch is operated, an insulated jumper conducts current to the contact diagonally opposite. Left—First position. Right—Second position.

A dimmer switch of the type shown should not be used to control wall outlets, fluorescent lights, appliances, or motor-driven equipment.

Note: Switches illustrated and described in this unit are typical examples of switches commonly used. Numerous other switches are available.

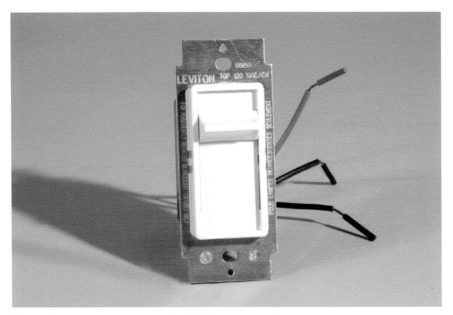

Figure 5-14. Dimmer switch with sliding knob.

Review Questions

Please do not write in the text. Place your answers on a separate sheet of paper.

1. A single-pole switch has _____ terminals and controls the electrical circuit from _____ location.
2. Three-way switches have _____ terminals and control the electrical circuit from _____ locations.
3. Four-way switches have _____ terminals and control the electrical circuit from _____ locations.
4. A mercury-operated switch is completely silent because there are no _____ _____ to snap or click.
5. *True or False?* The three kinds of canopy switches are the tumbler, feed through, and the pull chain.
6. When using a 4-way switch, it is necessary to use two _____ switches in the circuit.
7. A dimmer switch should never be used to control:
   a. _____
   b. _____
   c. _____
   d. _____

Wireless light switches can be placed anywhere in a room without worrying about running wires to the switch. A battery powered remote controls a special socket that can be placed up to 50 ft. away. (Lamson & Sessions)

Unit 6
Outlet Receptacles

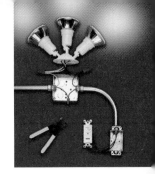

Receptacle Types

Receptacles, often called outlets, are used to supply electricity for portable appliances and devices. Among the appliances and devices are lamps, microwave ovens, toasters, televisions, radios, personal computers, and power tools.

Figure 6-1 shows an older type of receptacle without a grounding terminal. Such receptacles can only be used in older systems when they have no grounding system. The NEC allows a ground fault circuit interrupter to be used in place of the nongrounding type receptacle as long as it is marked "No Equipment Ground".

Figure 6-1. Duplex outlet without grounding terminal.

Figure 6-2 shows a duplex outlet with a green hex head screw terminal for a grounding wire. A *grounding terminal* provides a connection for a grounding conductor. This safety device bleeds off current to prevent shock in case of an electrical short. A green grounding wire or a bare wire is connected to the green hex head.

The duplex outlet also has a break-off fin. When the metal *break-off fin* is removed there is no connection between the two outlets. The receptacle can be used to provide outlets for two separate circuits.

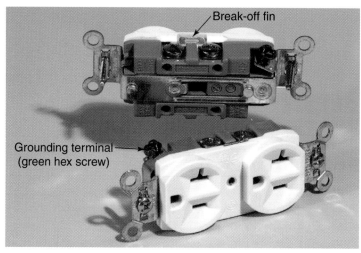

Figure 6-2. Duplex outlet. Note the green hex screw terminal for grounding wire and also the break-off fin.

A single receptacle with a U-shaped ground is shown in **Figure 6-3.** The green terminal connects to the bare or green-covered wire in the cable. Receptacles of this type are commonly used for dishwashers and other single-use installations.

Figure 6-3. Receptacle (240 V) for tandem blades and U-shaped ground.

A receptacle for three wires, 240 V is illustrated in **Figure 6-4.** Receptacles of this kind provide for easy connection and disconnection of equipment such as electric dryers and ranges.

Figure 6-5 illustrates a single receptacle (240 V) for horizontal and vertical blades and a U-shaped ground. This receptacle is for large air conditioners, heavy power tools, garden equipment, etc. The green terminal connects to the bare (or green covered) wire in the cable.

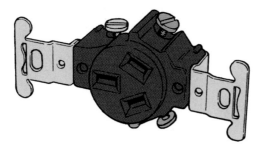

Figure 6-4. Receptacle for three wires, 240 V.

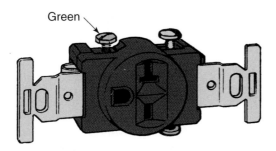

Figure 6-5. Receptacle (240 V) for horizontal and vertical blades and U-shaped ground.

Figure 6-6. No-shock outlet with self-closing openings.

A no-shock safety duplex outlet is shown in **Figure 6-6.** In this receptacle, self-closing outlets prevent small children from inserting metal objects and getting a shock. To use a no-shock type outlet, insert the plug, twist clockwise a quarter turn, and push in the plug. When the plug is pulled out, the rotary cap snaps shut. Weatherproof receptacles for outdoor devices are shown in **Figure 6-7.**

In house wiring, provisions for telephones also should be made. Conduit or cable of an approved type should be installed that terminates in switch boxes at the locations where telephones are desired. A special wall connecting block (wall jack), left, **Figure 6-8,** is provided. The local telephone company should be consulted for complete instructions prior to construction. Figure 6-8 also shows a special wall plate used for television. TV lead-in cable is run from the antenna, satellite dish, or cable system to a box at the back of the plate, without the use of conduit.

A plastic safety cap for wall outlets, which can be used to keep children from inserting dangerous metal objects into outlets, is shown in **Figure 6-9.**

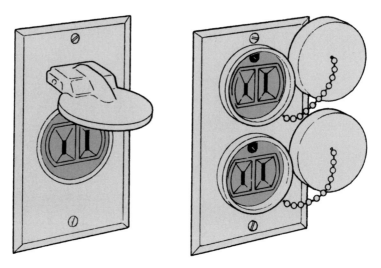

Figure 6-7. Weatherproof receptacles. Left—Outlet without grounding terminal. Right—Grounded duplex receptacle.

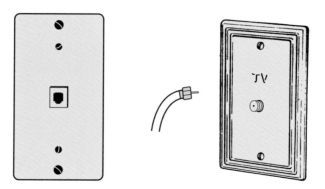

Figure 6-8. Left—Wall jack for telephone. Right—Plate for TV.

Figure 6-9. Safety cap.

Review Questions

Please do not write in the text. Place your answers on a separate sheet of paper.

Match the description of the outlet receptacle in the list on the left with the proper use in the list on the right.

a. Duplex outlet without grounding terminal.

b. Tandem blades and U-shaped ground 240 V outlet.

c. Three-wire 240 V outlet.

d. Horizontal and vertical blades 240 V outlet system.

e. Self-closing rotary cap outlet.

f. Special wall plate for antenna lead-in cable.

1. _____ Dryers, ranges, etc.

2. _____ Large air conditioners, heavy tools, garden equipment.

3. _____ Replacement in non-grounded system.

4. _____ Television signal reception.

5. _____ No-shock, prevents children inserting metal objects.

6. _____ Air conditioners.

Switches and outlets come in a variety of shapes and styles.
(Pass & Seymour/Legrand)

Unit 7
Electrician's Tools and Equipment

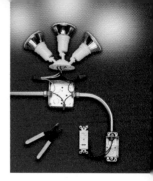

In this unit we will discuss tools that will help you with your house wiring jobs.

Pliers

Pliers are available with both insulated and uninsulated handles. Insulated handle pliers should be used when working on or near hot wires. The handle insulation should not be considered sufficient protection alone. Other safety precautions must be observed. Several types of pliers are shown in **Figure 7-1.**

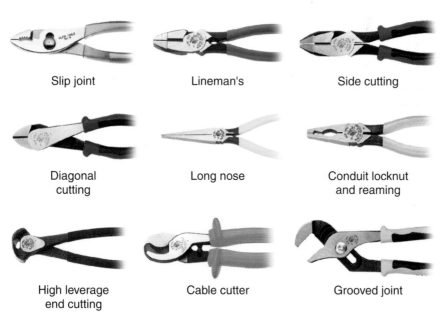

Slip joint

Lineman's

Side cutting

Diagonal cutting

Long nose

Conduit locknut and reaming

High leverage end cutting

Cable cutter

Grooved joint

Figure 7-1. Typical pliers and cutters used in house wiring. (Klein Tools, Inc.)

Screwdrivers

Screwdrivers come in various sizes and with several tip shapes, **Figure 7-2.** Screwdrivers used by electricians should have insulated handles. For safe and efficient use, screwdriver tips should be kept square and sharp. In selecting a screwdriver for a particular job, the width of the screwdriver tip should match the width of the screw slot.

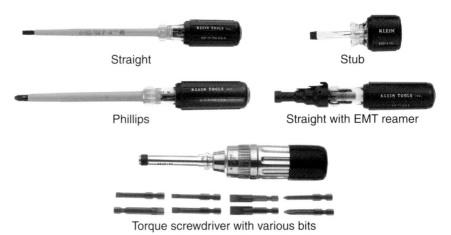

Straight   Stub

Phillips   Straight with EMT reamer

Torque screwdriver with various bits

Figure 7-2. Types of screwdrivers used in house wiring. (Klein Tools, Inc.)

Drilling Equipment

Drilling equipment is needed to make holes in building structures for passage of conduit and wire in both new and old construction. See **Figures 7-3** and **7-4.**

Figure 7-3. Power drill.

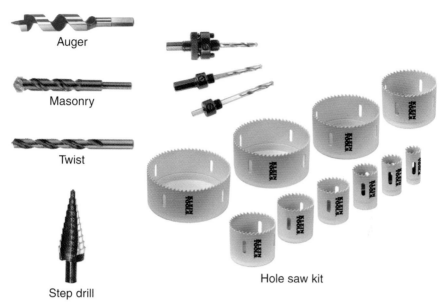

Figure 7-4. Variety of drill bits. (Klein Tools, Inc.)

Sawing and Cutting Tools

Hand saws commonly used by electricians include the crosscut, keyhole, and hacksaw. Power saws commonly used by electricians include the circular saw and the saber saw. See **Figures 7-5** and **7-6.**

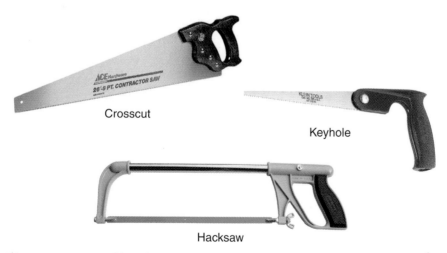

Figure 7-5. Typical hand saws. (Ace Hardware Corp. and Klein Tools, Inc.)

Circular saw

Reciprocating saw

Figure 7-6. Typical power saws. (Makita Corp.)

Soldering Equipment

Soldering is one method of forming electrical connections such as splices and taps (connections made to wire at points other than the ends). There are also some solderless connectors that can also be used. Typical equipment available for soldering is shown in **Figure 7-7.**

Multipurpose Tool

Figure 7-8 shows a tool that can be used as a pair of pliers, to cut and strip insulation from wire, to crimp terminals, and to cut screws.

Hammers

Hammers are used with chisels, for nailing, and for fitting. **Figure 7-9** shows a carpenter's claw hammer, lineman's hammer, and a machinist's ball-peen hammer.

Measuring Tools

To measure wire length, opening sizes, conduit, and other items, the electrician finds considerable use for measuring tools such as the extension rule, push-pull tape rule, and a steel tape, **Figure 7-10.**

Fish Wire or Tape

Fish tapes are used to pull (fish) wires through conduits in new work and through wall openings in old work. These tapes are made

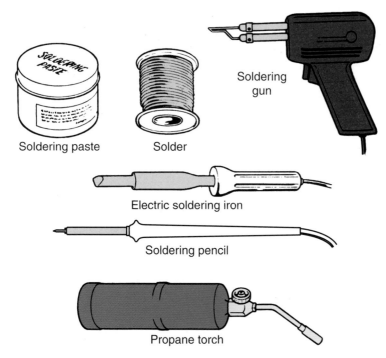

Soldering gun

Soldering paste

Solder

Electric soldering iron

Soldering pencil

Propane torch

Figure 7-7. Soldering equipment.

Figure 7-8. Multipurpose tool. (Klein Tools, Inc.)

of tempered spring steel and come in lengths to suit various requirements. See **Figure 7-11.**

Wire pulling lubricant or compound (usually a creamy textured
compound with wax base) is used to make wire pulling easier.

Miscellaneous Tools and Equipment

Additional tools and equipment needed in handling house
wiring jobs include: conduit benders, pipe cutters, test lights,

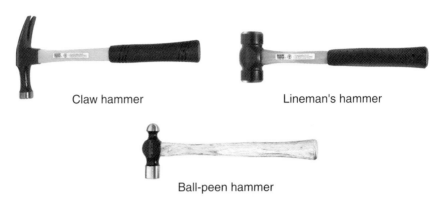

Claw hammer   Lineman's hammer

Ball-peen hammer

Figure 7-9. Hammers used in house wiring. (Klein Tools, Inc.)

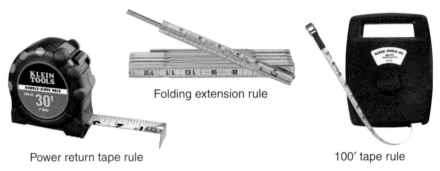

Folding extension rule

Power return tape rule   100′ tape rule

Figure 7-10. Useful measuring tools. (Klein Tools, Inc.)

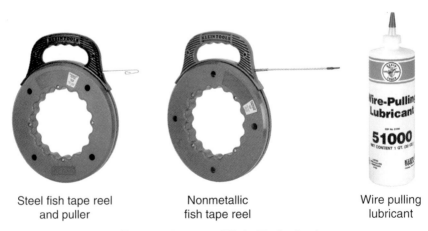

Steel fish tape reel   Nonmetallic   Wire pulling
and puller   fish tape reel   lubricant

Figure 7-11. Wire pulling equipment. (Klein Tools, Inc.)

reamers, and BX cutters. See **Figures 7-12** and **7-13.** Other useful items include: wrenches, files, fuse pullers, pipe vises, taps and dies for threading conduit, plumb bobs for establishing true vertical lines, flashlights, test equipment, wire gauges, and powder-actuated stud drivers.

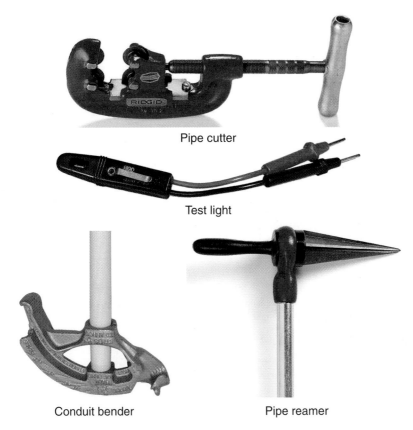

Pipe cutter

Test light

Conduit bender   Pipe reamer

Figure 7-12. Miscellaneous tools and equipment used in house wiring. (Klein Tools, Inc.)

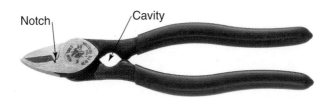

Figure 7-13. BX cutter. Notch is designed for stripping off insulation. (Klein Tools, Inc.)

Review Questions

Please do not write in the text. Place your answers on a separate sheet of paper.

Identify the tools shown below.

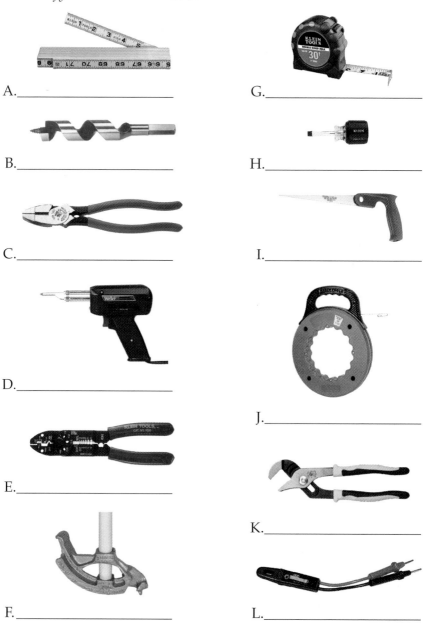

A._____

B._____

C._____

D._____

E._____

F._____

G._____

H._____

I._____

J._____

K._____

L._____

Unit 8
Working Safely

In house wiring, both the worker and the employer must assume important responsibilities to prevent on-the-job injuries. The employer is responsible for providing proper equipment, equipment maintenance, and safe working conditions. Final responsibility for safe working practices rests with the worker.

Shock Effects

If a 60 hertz alternating current is passed through a person, from hand to hand or from hand to foot, the usual effects are:

- ❏ At about 1 milliampere (0.001 ampere) the shock may be felt.
- ❏ At about 10 milliamperes (0.010 ampere) the shock may be severe enough to paralyze muscles so a person is unable to release the conductor.
- ❏ At approximately 100 milliamperes (0.100 ampere) the shock may be fatal if it lasts for one second or more.

The amount of shock depends on conditions at the time and place of contact. If a live wire is contacted while you are standing on a dry wooden floor, the shock may be negligible. If you are standing on a damp floor, your body may become a conductor that leads the current to the ground. A serious shock can result. Shock is far more severe when your hands are damp or wet because water or perspiration reduces the resistance of your body.

When an electric shock is received, the current can cause breathing to stop. If the shock is not too severe, breathing may resume after a short time, provided a sufficient supply of oxygen is furnished to the body through CPR.

Freeing a Victim

The first person to reach a shocked worker should cut off the current **if this can be done quickly.** If not, the victim should be removed from contact with the energized equipment.

Determine whether the live wire can be removed from the victim, or whether the victim should be pulled away from the wire. Your bare hands **must not** be used to pull the victim away. Use a dry board, dry rope, leather belt, coat, overalls, or some other nonconductor. Be sure to stand on a nonconducting surface.

Call the local emergency number (usually 911) and give CPR until a paramedic or other competent person familiar with lifesaving methods arrives.

Figure 8-1. Electricity packs a terrific wallop. Use your head. Think! Stay alive!

Safety Suggestions

The following suggestions will help prevent accidents and injuries to you and your coworkers.

❏ Do not tap into live wires. Find the switch or circuit breaker, and cut off the current before starting to work on the circuit.

❏ When cutting flexible cable with a hacksaw, be sure to hold the cable against a solid object—not against your knee.

❏ Remember, your eyes are a priceless possession. Protect your eyes. Wear goggles or a face shield when there is a possibility of being injured by flying chips or electric flashes.

❑ Use all tools correctly. Make sure all tools are in good working condition. When there is a danger of shock, use tools with insulated handles—nonmetallic tools if available. Use dry cloth measuring tapes.

❑ Handle and lift objects carefully. When lifting, bend your knees and keep your back as nearly upright as possible.

❑ Periodically run a current leakage check on portable power tools. Also check the tools for proper grounding, to make sure they are safe to use.

❑ Check service outlets for polarity and proper grounding.

❑ Keep the floor around your working area clean, dry, and free from litter.

❑ Never use a lamp or appliance if the insulation on the cord is worn and ragged. Replace, don't splice, a broken cord. Discard "beat up" extension cords.

❑ Do not remove a plug from an outlet by jerking on the cord. Pull on the plug.

❑ Before working on electrical equipment, all rings, wristwatches, bracelets, and similar metal items should be removed. Be sure there are no exposed zippers or metal buttons on your clothing.

❑ Do not throw a circuit breaker or replace a fuse until the cause of the trouble has been found and corrected.

❑ Burns can result from contact with a hot soldering iron or gun. When soldering, be sure to place the hot iron where it is not likely to be touched by an unsuspecting person.

❑ Many batteries contain acid electrolyte. Drops of the acid can burn your hands and eat holes in your clothing. Battery acid can be neutralized by using a solution of baking soda and water.

❑ On electrical wiring jobs (on live or near live electrical parts), two people should always work together.

❑ In case of injury, even minor, be sure to get first aid.

❑ When working around electricity, be *cautious* but not *scared*. Remember that safety and thoughtfulness are closely related.

❑ Remember the ABC's of house wiring—Always Be Careful.

Review Questions

Please do not write in the text. Place your answers on a separate sheet of paper.

1. *True or False?* You can tap into live wires if you use tools with insulated handles.
2. *True or False?* When lifting, bend your knees, keep your back as nearly upright as possible.
3. *True or False?* When a lamp cord breaks, it is wise to splice it.
4. *True or False?* The best way to remove a plug from an outlet is by pulling on the cord.
5. *True or False?* You should not reset a circuit breaker or replace a fuse until the cause of the trouble has been found and corrected.
6. *True or False?* When working on electrical equipment, keep your wristwatch on so you can tell what time it is.
7. *True or False?* Battery acid may be neutralized by using a solution of baking soda and water.

Unit 9
Service
Requirements

Electrical service for today's home should provide for both 120- and 240-volt circuits.

Two power line wires running to a residential service entrance indicate 120-volt service. Three wires indicate 240-volt service is available. One wire is a neutral or grounded wire; the other two are *hot* wires, **Figure 9-1.** Lamps ordinarily used in the home and most plug-in appliances use 120-volt electricity. Many major appliances—electric ranges, electric clothes dryers, air conditioners, etc.—need 240 volts.

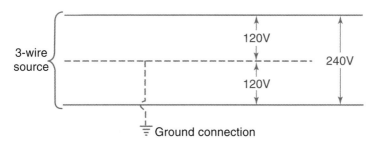

Figure 9-1. A 240-volt circuit is a combination of two 120-volt circuits.

Service entrance conductors are connected to a main switch, circuit breaker, or fuse. The service entrance equipment serves as the junction point from which electricity is dispatched to various parts of the house by a number of smaller wires. These are called **branch circuits.**

Service Entrance Ratings

Service entrance equipment is rated in amperes, just like appliances or lightbulbs. The equipment must have sufficient capacity to accommodate the maximum amount of current that will be used at one time—both now and in the future.

Today, in most areas, 100-ampere service, which may be provided by using No. 3 or No. 2 copper conductors with RHW insulation and a service entrance panel of 100-ampere capacity, is the minimum recommended for new homes.

To install 150- or 200-ampere service, No. 1/0 or 3/0 (with type RHW insulation) 3-wire service with a 150- or 200-ampere service panel is used, **Figure 9-2.** These service levels are desirable where full "housepower" is required. In homes equipped with an electric water heater, range, dryer, or central air conditioning, and the usual number of small appliances, 150-ampere service is suggested as a minimum. If the home is to be heated by electricity, or if the owner requires more than the normal quantity of appliances, 200-ampere service is usually needed.

To determine the maximum wattage available, multiply the amperage rating by the voltage. With a 100-ampere service, multiply 100×240 giving 24,000 watts or volt-amperes. For wattage available with 150-ampere service, multiply 150×240 giving 36,000 watts or volt-amperes. A 200-ampere service will make available 200×240, or 48,000 watts or volt-amperes.

Figure 9-3 lists a number of appliance wattages. The wattages shown are typical. Actual wattage ratings for different brands of appliances vary considerably. By adding together wattages of appliances and lamps that may be used at the same time and the wattages of appliances that may be added in the future, you can get a good idea of service requirement needs for a particular home.

Electrical Symbols

Electrical symbols, **Figure 9-4,** are the electrician's system of "shorthand" used on building plans. They provide a simple way to show the electrical service to be provided and where outlets and switches are to be installed. The use of electrical symbols is shown in **Figure 9-5.**

Branch Circuits

Modern house wiring circuits can be divided into three general classes:

- ❑ General purpose circuits.
- ❑ Appliance circuits.
- ❑ Individual circuits.

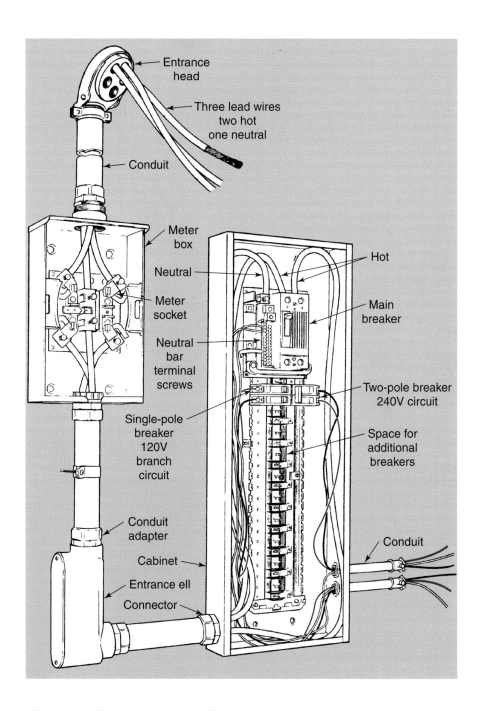

Figure 9-2. Service entrance with 200-ampere capacity.

Appliance	Typical wattage (volt amperes)	Appliance	Typical wattage (volt amperes)
Air conditioner (room)	1200	Hot plate	1500
Air conditioner (central)	5000	Ironer	1650
Attic fan	400	Lamps, each bulb	25-200
Automatic toaster	1200	Mechanism for fuel-fired	
Automatic washer	700	heating plant	800
Broiler	1000	Oil burner	250
Built-in ventilating fan	400	Portable fan	100
Coffeemaker	1000	Portable heater	1650
Egg cooker	600	Radio	100
Deep fryer	1320	Ranges, electric	12000
Dehumidifier	350	Refrigerator	200
Dishwasher-disposer	1500	Rotisserie	1380
Dry iron or steam iron	1000	Roaster	1380
Electric blanket	200	Sandwich grill	1320
Electric clock	2	Saw, radial	750
Clothes dryer	9000	TV	350
Freezer	350	Vacuum cleaner	300
Fluorescent lights		Ventilating fan	400
(each tube)	15-40	Waffle iron	1300
Griddle	1000	Waste disposer	500
Hair dryer	1000	Water heater	3500
Heat or sun lamp	300	Water pump	700

Figure 9-3. Typical appliance wattages.

General purpose circuits should be used for lighting outlets in all rooms and for convenience outlets in all rooms except the kitchen, dining area, and laundry. General purpose circuits should be provided on the basis of one 20-ampere 120-volt circuit for not more than each 500 sq. ft. of floor space. Each 20-ampere circuit wired with No. 12 wire will have a capacity of 2400 volt-amperes. Fifteen-ampere circuits with No. 14 wire will provide 1750 volt-amperes (same as watts).

Convenience outlets with duplex outlets should be provided along the wall every 12 ft. and as code requires on cabinet tops. Outlets on general purpose circuits should be divided equally among the circuits.

A *split-circuit wiring* arrangement, which provides two separate circuits in each outlet box, is shown in Figure 12-13. Such wiring is desirable if there is a need to balance a load of heavy appliances.

Appliance circuits are used in the kitchen area and the laundry room. There should be a minimum of two 20-ampere circuits (using No. 12 wire) in the kitchen and dining area. There should be one 20-ampere circuit in the laundry area. In the kitchen counter work area, convenience outlets for the appliance circuits should be

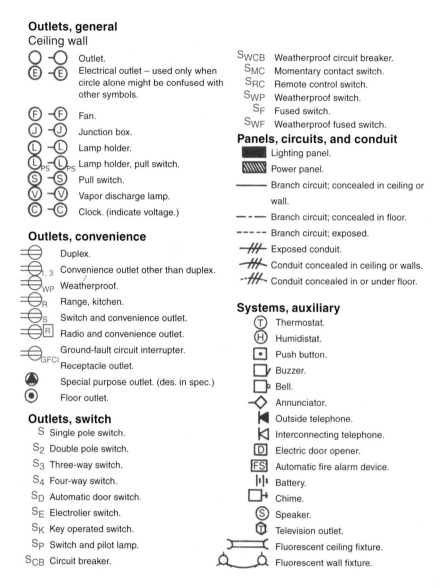

Figure 9-4. Electrical symbols with which you should become familiar.

provided so that no point along the wall is more than 24 in. (610 mm) from an outlet. If more than one heavy-duty appliance will be connected to the circuit, using No. 10 wire is advisable.

Individual circuits are used for major electrical appliances. Wire sizes and types of circuit breakers or fuses required for circuits serving individual pieces of major electrical equipment,

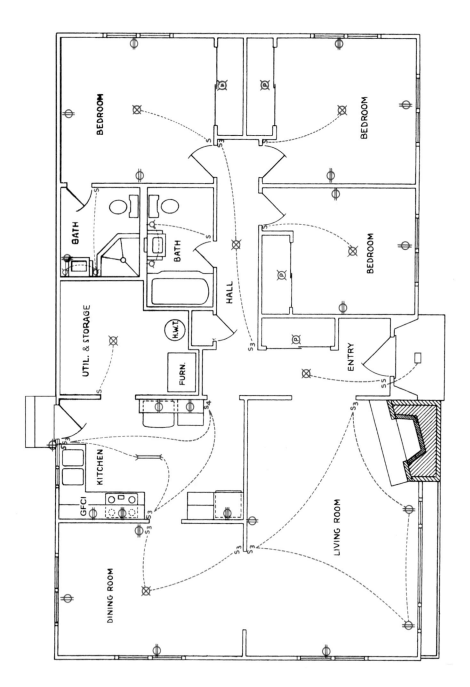

Figure 9-5. Residential floor plan in which symbols shown in Figure 9-4 are used.

such as ranges, water heaters, air conditioners, and space heaters, depend on the amperage rating of the appliances which are to be installed.

Figure 9-6 shows a typical hookup for an electric range or dryer. A 3-wire, No. 6 cable is run from a 50-ampere circuit breaker in the main service panel, which is run to a heavy-duty wall receptacle. A flexible 3-wire cord or "pigtail" is connected to the range or dryer terminals. The other end of the cord has a 3-prong plug that fits into a receptacle. This permits the range or dryer to be easily disconnected. The metal frame of the appliance should be grounded to the neutral terminal.

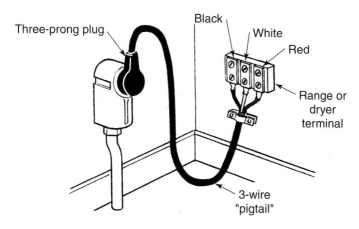

Figure 9-6. Typical electric range or dryer hookup. The neutral wire is grounded to the frame of the appliance, generally with a grounding strap.

An appliance circuit can be designed to supply both 120- and 240-volt current. Electric ranges usually operate on 240 volts at high heat and 120 volts at low heat. Dryers generally require 240 volts for heating and 120 volts for lights and motors.

Building Code Example

Additional information on the requirements of an adequate wiring system for a modern dwelling can be obtained by studying your city's electrical code.

Review Questions

Please do not write in the text. Place your answers on a separate sheet of paper.

1. Electrical service for today's modern home should provide for both _____ and _____ volt circuits.
2. A residential service entrance with _____ power line wires indicates 120-volt service.
3. *True or False?* Three-wire 240-volt service uses one neutral or ground wire and two hot wires.
4. Service entrance conductors are connected to:
   a. _____
   b. _____
   c. _____
5. Today, the minimum recommended service for new homes is _____ amperes.
6. To determine the maximum wattage available, multiply the _____ rating by the voltage.
7. General purpose circuits should be used for lighting outlets in all rooms and for convenience outlets in all rooms except the _____, _____, and _____.
8. Split-circuit wiring provides _____ separate circuits in each outlet box.
9. Wire sizes and types of circuit breakers or fuses required for circuits serving individual pieces of major electrical equipment will depend on the _____ of the appliances to be installed.

Unit 10
Basic Wiring Systems

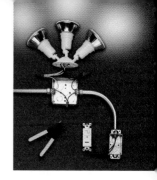

In modern house wiring, the basic systems commonly used involve sheathed nonmetallic cable, armored cable, and metal conduit.

Sheathed Nonmetallic Cable

Nonmetallic cable is often used on house wiring jobs where the codes permit. It is easy to install, particularly where it is necessary to "snake" the cable through the walls.

Installation of nonmetallic cable is shown in **Figure 10-1.** At the cable ends, strip off the covering allowing at least 8 in. of insulated wire for making connections. Fasten the connector to the outside of the cable cover, and insert the cable through the knockout hole of the box. The connector is designed to tightly grip the cable. Screw on the locknut on the inside tightly.

Run the cable through holes drilled in center of joists or strap the cable no farther apart than 4 1/2 ft. on supporting surfaces such as studs, joists, walls, or the ceiling. Where the cable runs across joists or through open spaces, support should be provided by running a board (usually 1 × 4) to which the cable is strapped.

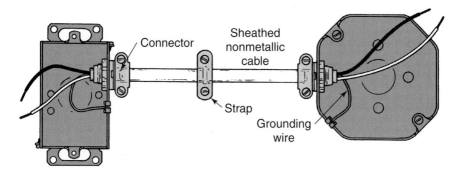

Figure 10-1. Installing nonmetallic cable.

In roof areas or attics, run the cable across the top of floor beams or across the faces of rafters. Protect the cable by using guard strips.

Secure the cable every 4 1/2 ft. with straps, ties, or staples. Also, strap the cable within 12 in. of each switch and outlet. In new buildings, straps must be used for all runs whether exposed or concealed. In old work, fasteners must be used for all exposed runs, but they are not necessary for concealed runs.

Often, codes require a ground wire when using nonmetalic cable, **Figure 10-2.** By using a ground wire, you will have a system that is continuously grounded. This will reduce the danger of shock if some metal appliance case should accidentally become charged with electricity (shorted).

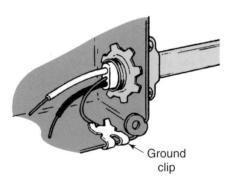

Ground
clip

Figure 10-2. Nonmetallic cable. Ground wire is connected to the box.

Caution: **Before starting on any house wiring job, check codes applicable to the job. See to it that all code restrictions are carefully observed.**

Installing Armored Cable

Installing armored cable is shown in Figures 10-3 to 10-7. If using a hacksaw to cut the metal armor, **Figure 10-3A,** place the cable on a solid base and saw through one section of armor. Twist to break. Use shears to trim off sharp corners. Allow a length of at least 8 in. of insulated wire for making connections in the box.

The paper wrapping is removed to expose the insulation covering the wire conductor. Carefully strip off the insulation using the multipurpose stripping tool shown in Figure 7-8, or a BX cutter. See **Figure 10-3B.**

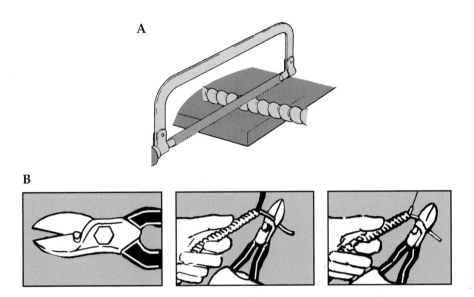

Figure 10-3. A. Using hacksaw to cut armored cable. B. Using notch on BX cutter to strip insulation.

Cutting armored cable with metal-cutting shears is shown in **Figure 10-4.** First, bend the armor sharply to buckle it. Then, grip the cable on both sides of the buckled point and twist against the direction of the spiral to open one turn of cable winding. Cut with snips and trim off sharp corners. Removing armor exposes water-repellent paper wrapping.

Insert an anti-short bushing, a code requirement, between the paper and the wires with the bushing turned to cover sharp edges. See **Figure 10-5.** Remove the excess paper. Slip the connector with the locknut removed over the wires and armor. Make sure the cable is inserted into the connector as far as possible (the anti-short bushing must touch front of connector), then tighten the screw. See **Figure 10-6.** In examining the end of the bushing that fits in the box, you will notice "peep" holes through which the bushing can be seen.

Figure 10-4. Cutting cable with metal-cutting shears.

Figure 10-5. Inserting anti-short bushing between the armor and the wires.

Electrical inspectors use these holes in checking to make sure the bushings have been used.

Some armored cable has a bare ground wire. This should be bent back against armor on the outside and fastened to the screw of the connector, **Figure 10-7.** The ground wire, which has less resistance than armored cable, provides a ground connection through the cable from box to box. This is required by some building codes.

Armored cable must be supported by a staple or strap every 4 1/2 ft., and within 12 in. of each outlet box, junction box, cabinet, or fitting except for concealed runs in old work where it is impractical to use straps or staples for support.

Caution: **All wiring connections and splices must be made inside electrical boxes.**

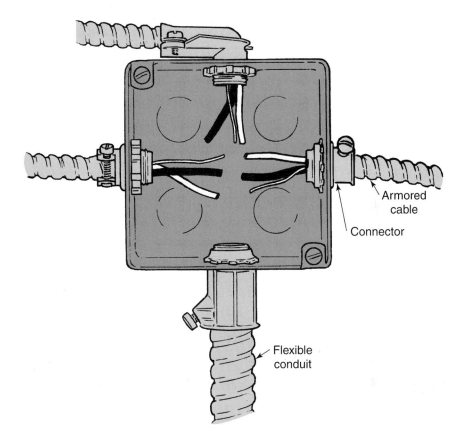

Figure 10-6. Top and Sides. Using three different types of armored cable box connectors. Bottom. Flexible conduit (greenfield) before wires are installed. In an actual wiring job, the ends of the insulated wires in box would be at least 6 in. long.

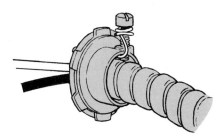

Figure 10-7. Attaching BX cable grounding wire to the screw of the connector. Note: Set screw connectors are NOT to be used on aluminum armored cable.

Installing Metal Conduit

Thinwall conduit, also called electrical metallic tubing, provides considerable protection for current-carrying wires and is required in many localities.

To select conduit, refer to the tables in Chapter 9 and Annex C of the *Code.* In general, 1/2 in. conduit will carry four 14 AWG wires or three 12 AWG wires; 3/4 in. conduit will carry four 10 AWG wires, five 12 AWG wires, or three 8 AWG wires.

Thinwall conduit comes in 10 ft. lengths that must be joined by threadless connectors. See **Figures 10-8** and **10-9.** Conduit may be cut to length with an ordinary hacksaw using a fine tooth blade (32 teeth per inch). Use a reamer or a round file to remove sharp edges and burrs. See **Figure 10-10.**

Figure 10-8. The wall thickness of 1/2 in. dia. thinwall conduit is 0.042 in.

A   B

Figure 10-9. Using couplings on thinwall conduit. A—Setscrew B—Compression

Figure 10-10. This ramer is attached to a screwdriver. (Klein Tools, Inc.)

Use a conduit bender to bend thinwall conduit as shown in **Figure 10-11.** To make a smooth, even bend, take short bites. Be sure to follow instructions provided by the manufacturer. A little experimenting with a bender will enable you to get the knack of using it. Do not have more than four quarter bends in a run of conduit from one box to another. Avoid short bends.

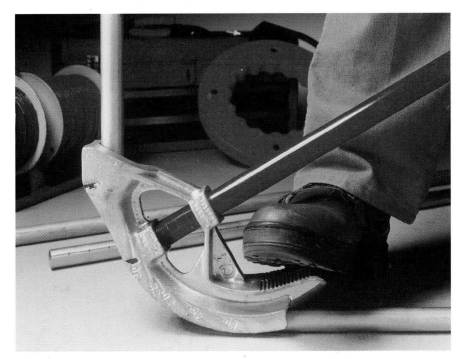

Figure 10-11. Using conduit bender. (GB Electrical Inc.)

In areas where conduit runs along the side of a joist or stud, it should be supported every 6 to 8 ft. with a pipe strap or clamp. In areas where conduit runs horizontally across wall studs, notches should be cut, which are then protected with steel plates. Holes can also be drilled to provide a channel for the conduit, **Figure 10-12.** Check the local building code.

The notching of studs can be eliminated, to a considerable extent, by running the conduit across subfloors. When the conduit is in place, furring strips are run up to the conduit. Finish flooring is laid over the furring strips, **Figure 10-13.**

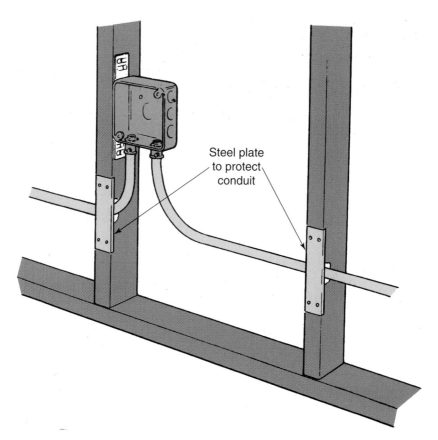

Figure 10-12. Wall studs are notched to provide channels for conduit.

Threadless connectors are used to connect the conduit to the metal boxes. Insert the conduit through the box knockout opening, and tighten the nut on the inside.

In new work, the conduit is put in place before the house is completely built. After the walls have been finished, wires are run through the conduit and connected to switches and outlets.

Rigid conduit, **Figure 10-14,** comes in both black and galvanized types. It looks very much like water pipe. The principle difference between rigid conduit and water pipe is that the conduit is softer, making it easier to bend. Rigid conduit should be closely inspected for sharp projections on the inside that might cut the insulation from wires when pulling them through the conduit.

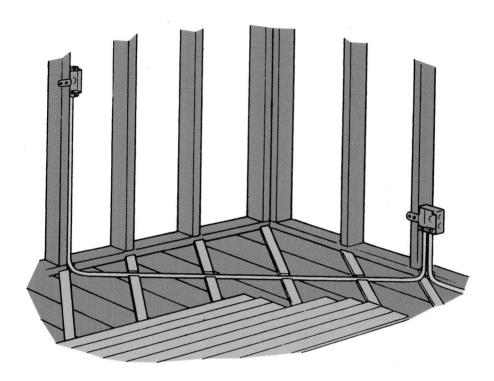

Figure 10-13. Running conduit across subfloor.

Figure 10-14. Rigid conduit is threaded like water pipe.

Rigid conduit comes in the same sizes as water pipe: 1/2 in., 3/4 in., 1 in., 1 1/4 in., and larger. Note that the measurements given are inside measurements. Rigid conduit can be cut and threaded with the same tools used for water pipe.

Protective Grounding System

The modern house wiring system has an equipment grounding system. This system is independent of the grounded neutral (white wire). It provides an unbroken electrical path from a tool or appliance, through the receptacle, to the branch circuit, through the entrance panel, and from there to ground. An electrical short in a tool or appliance will pass harmlessly to ground instead of causing an electrical shock.

A grounded receptacle has the usual two slots plus a third U-shaped slot that is grounded to the rest of the circuit. See **Figure 10-15**. The third prong of an electrical plug is connected to the metal case of the tool or appliance by a third wire.

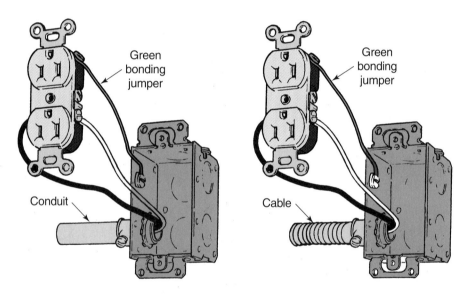

Green bonding jumper

Green bonding jumper

Conduit

Cable

Figure 10-15. Connecting grounding wire to box.

In the receptacle, the third opening is electrically connected to a third terminal. The terminal screw is color-coded green.

The grounding system provides for continuity from outlet box to ground by:

1. Using metal boxes and metallic conduit as conductors.
2. Using metal boxes and a third (base) grounding wire in electrical cable. Connecting the third wire to the metal outlet box gives continuity. On a conduit system the conduit itself provides the ground if it runs back to the entrance panel.

Continuity between a properly grounded outlet box using either cable or conduit and the grounding circuit of the receptacle should be established by using a bonding jumper between the box and the grounding screw of the receptacle. Look again at Figure 10-15.

The jumper is usually not required if the construction and installation of the receptacle is such that direct metal-to-metal contact is established between the receptacle (of approved type) and the box in which it is installed.

Ground-Fault Circuit Interrupters

Ground-fault circuit interrupters are commonly referred to as *GFCIs.* The GFCIs are connected between the power line and the tool or appliance being used. These devices sense ground (leakage) currents. When the currents entering and leaving the circuit are not identical, they automatically turn off the primary power within 25 to 30 milliseconds.

GFCIs should be installed wherever moisture is present or there is any chance that a tool or appliance being used might contact a grounded metal surface. All 120-volt single-phase 15- and 20-ampere receptacle outlets installed outdoors, in bathrooms, and at kitchen counters need to have ground-fault circuit protection.

Arc Fault Circuit Interrupters

The National Electrical Code requires that all bedroom circuits be protected by an *arc fault circuit interrupter (AFCI).* Any circuit with a receptacle, light fixture, or other device in a bedroom or closet must be protected by an AFCI. AFCIs are designed to prevent fires by stopping the flow of electricity when arcing is detected in the circuit. AFCIs provide protection from faulty wiring, damaged extension cords, and defective appliances.

While there are receptacle-type GFCIs, there are no receptacle-type AFCIs. The AFCI breaker must be located in the electrical panel. This provides protection for the entire circuit.

Review Questions

Please do not write in the text. Place your answers on a separate sheet of paper.

1. Before starting any house wiring job, check the _____ applicable to the job.
2. When making connections with nonmetallic cable, strip off the _____ leaving at least 8 in. of insulated wire.
3. *True or False?* When fastening nonmetallic cable to supports, do not use staples.
4. A continuously grounded system will reduce the danger of _____.
5. Armored cable can be cut using a(n) _____ or _____.
6. _____ are used to protect wires from sharp edges on the ends of armored cable.
7. *True or False?* All wiring connections and splices in nonmetallic and armored cable must be made inside metal boxes.
8. Thinwall conduit may be cut with a(n) _____ and joined using _____ connectors.
9. *True or False?* Using a conduit bender, it is good practice to make up to nine bends in a run of conduit from one box to another.
10. Rigid conduit can be cut and threaded with the same tools used to cut and thread _____.

Raceway allows additional outlets to be installed in a room without having to punch holes in the walls. (The Wiremold Co.)

Unit 11
Basic Wiring
Procedures

In 120-volt house wiring there are two wires; a *hot* power-carrying wire, and a *neutral* grounded wire. See **Figure 11-1.**

Figure 11-1. Two-wire, 120-volt circuit consists of one hot wire and one neutral wire.

Color Coding or Polarizing

Wires throughout the system are identified by color to make sure that hot, or current-carrying, wires are connected to hot wires, and that the neutral or grounded wires run in continuous, uninterrupted circuits.

To maintain the identity of the conductors, the *National Electrical Code* requires that the neutral or grounded wire be white or natural gray. The hot wire can be black or any color other than green, gray, or white. Using a green wire in a protective grounding system is described in Unit 10.

A white or gray wire is actually a current-carrying conductor for the 120-volt circuit too, even though it is called a neutral or grounded wire. The white wire is a very important part of the wiring system. It must be insulated throughout its length, and should be treated with the same respect as the hot wire.

The white or gray neutral wire must be grounded at the main switch. This means that it is connected to the earth through another conductor. The neutral wire must also run to each 120-volt outlet without being interrupted by fuses or switches.

The grounded wire from the box to the water main need not be insulated. The minimum size ground wire that can be used is No. 8. Additional information on ground wire size can be obtained from the table on page 154. In connecting the ground to the cold water pipe, a jumper must be installed around the water meter, **Figure 11-2,** if the connection is made on the building side of the water meter (the side *not* coming into building from outside).

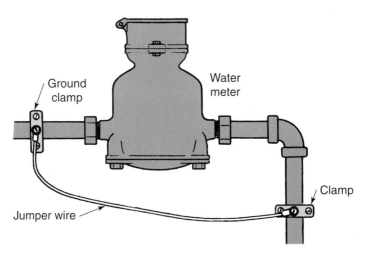

Figure 11-2. Jumper wire installed around water meter.

Three-Wire Circuit

A 3-wire circuit includes two hot (colored) wires and one (white or gray) neutral wire. Each colored wire provides 120 volts. Connecting the two colored wires, and a white wire to an appliance such as a range or water heater, provides 240 volts, **Figure 11-3.**

Figure 11-3. Three-wire circuit that provides 240 volts for appliance use.

Connecting Wires to Terminals

The black or hot wire should be connected to brass-colored terminals on receptacles, switches, fuse and circuit breaker terminals, and to black wires on lighting fixtures. The white or gray wires should be connected to the light or silver-colored terminals on all receptacles and to the white wires on lighting fixtures. See **Figure 11-4.**

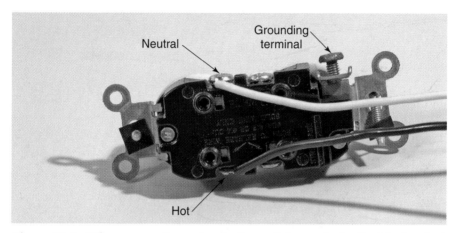

Figure 11-4. When connecting wires to the outlet receptacle, the black or hot wire should be connected to the brass-colored terminal and the white (neutral) wire to the light or silver-colored terminal.

Switches are always connected into the black wire. See **Figure 11-5.** In making a connection to a switch or receptacle terminal, remove about 7/8 in. of the insulation, (using wire stripping tool is easiest way) and connect with wire bent to form a clockwise loop, **Figure 11-6.** If insulation is removed with a knife, taper insulation at the end so the wire will not be nicked by the knife, **Figure 11-7.**

Using solderless connectors

In modern house wiring most soldering is eliminated by the use of solderless connectors (wire nuts), **Figure 11-8.** The connectors are made of insulating materials, so no taping is required. Twist the wires together, then screw the connector over the wires being sure no bare copper wire is exposed. Remember, all connections must be enclosed in electrical boxes.

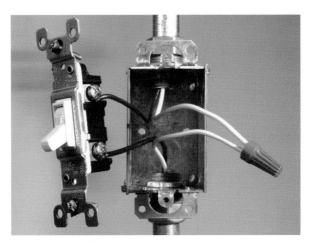

Figure 11-5. Both switch terminals are always connected into the hot wire.

Figure 11-6. The wire is bent clockwise to form a loop to make the connection to the terminals.

Figure 11-7. When using a knife to remove insulation, taper the insulation. This prevents nicking the wire with the knife and weakening it.

Figure 11-8. Solderless connectors. (GB Electrical Inc.)

Connections requiring soldering

Where solderless connectors are not used, wire splices and taps must be soldered. As shown in **Figure 11-9,** remove about 3 in. of insulation from each wire. Be sure the wires are bright and clean. Cross wires about 1 in. from insulation, then make 6 to 8 turns using your fingers and a pair of pliers. The connection must be tight and securely soldered using a non-acid flux or rosin-core solder. Heat should be applied to the wire joint so the heat from the wire melts the solder. Cover the joint with plastic tape, which does the work of both rubber and friction tapes. Be sure to provide insulation equal to the original wire insulation. (Splices must be housed in an electrical box.)

A *tap splice* (connecting end of wire at a point on a continuous wire) is shown in **Figure 11-10.** Clean the wires, and wrap the loose end around continuous wire. Solder the joint and then tape it.

Figure 11-11 shows a *pigtail splice.* The pigtail splice is sometimes used in outlet boxes to attach fixture leads or on other connections where there is no pull on the wires.

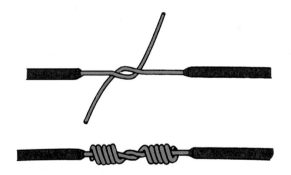

Figure 11-9. Splicing two wires.

Figure 11-10. Tap splice.

Figure 11-11. Pigtail splice.

Using a multipurpose tool to install a solderless terminal is shown in **Figure 11-12.** Plastic insulation is permanently bonded to the terminal.

Figure 11-12. Installing solderless terminal on heavy wire.

Installing Boxes

All wiring connections (wire ends and splices where insulation has been removed) and all switches and outlets must be enclosed in approved electrical *boxes.* The boxes should be located so they are accessible without damaging wall framing or covering.

Figure 11-13 shows switch and outlet receptacle boxes with side mounting brackets. **Figure 11-14** shows how an outlet box can be mounted between wall studs using a metal hanger. Remove the center knockout (machine punched circles that are not completely

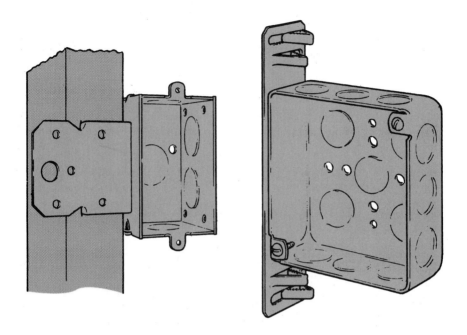

Figure 11-13. Left. Switch box with side mounting bracket. Nails are used to hold the box in place. Right. Square switch and receptacle box with side mounting bracket.

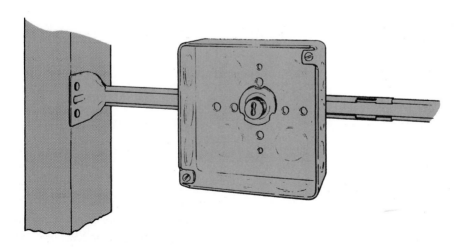

Figure 11-14. Mounting box between studs, using hanger.

severed) in the bottom of the box and slip the box over the fixture stud. Tighten the nut on the inside of the box.

The box should be mounted so the front edge is not more than 1/4 in. below the finished surface of the wall or ceiling. If the wall is made of combustible material, the front edge must extend out flush with the finished surface. Various covers are available for use with square boxes that will raise the front edge flush with the surface, **Figure 11-15.** See also Figure 4-8.

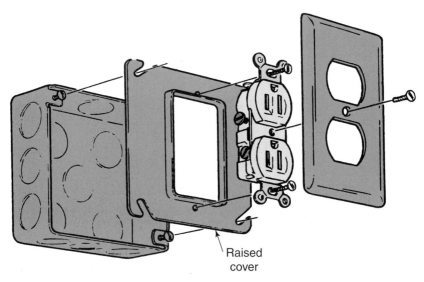

Raised cover

Figure 11-15. Square boxes should be used where extra space is needed for wires. Various types of raised covers are available.

Mounting Fixtures

Figure 11-16 shows a porcelain lampholder mounted directly onto a standard junction box.

In **Figure 11-17,** note the use of a *hickey* (reducer), which screws onto the threaded fixture stud and takes a threaded nipple. When a light fixture is installed, the nipple extends through the fixture. This is held in place by a cap screwed onto the nipple.

Providing fixture straps and threaded nipples for fixture support is shown in **Figure 11-18.**

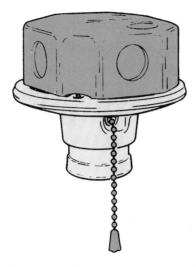

Figure 11-16. Porcelain lampholder mounted on junction box.

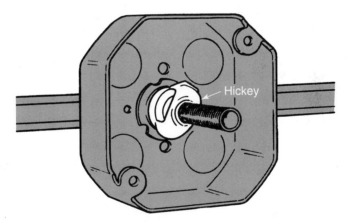

Figure 11-17. A hickey screwed onto threaded fixture stud takes a threaded nipple, which supports the fixture.

Provide box entry points for conduit and cable by removing knockouts. Use a beat-up screwdriver and hammer to tip circle. Use pliers to twist the knockouts off. Be careful not to remove more knockouts than necessary. Make the connection to the box as shown in **Figure 11-19.**

Ganging metal boxes is accomplished with metal switch boxes that are made so that they can be put together or *ganged* to provide

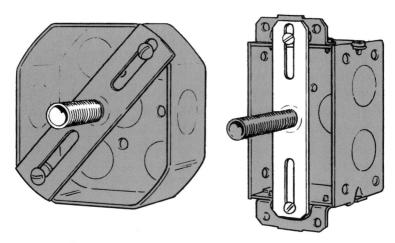

Figure 11-18. Fixture straps mounted on boxes take threaded nipples, which support fixtures.

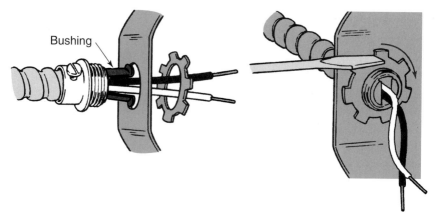

Figure 11-19. Connecting BX cable to a box. Use a bushing to protect insulation.

additional space. To connect the boxes, simply remove one side of each box, fit the boxes together, and tighten the screws.

Pulling Wire into Conduit

In new construction, wires should not be drawn through the conduit until the plastering has been finished. Make sure the wires conform to the standard color code. Use one black wire and one white or gray wire in a 2-wire circuit; use one black, one white or gray, and one red wire in a 3-wire circuit.

On short runs wires can usually be pushed through the conduit without using a fish tape. Where the run is long and several wires are to be inserted in the conduit, a fish tape will be needed, **Figure 11-20.** Fish tape is made of stiff, flexible steel, usually about 1/8 in. wide.

In using a fish tape, insert the end of the tape in the conduit. When the end emerges, attach wires to be pulled into the conduit, **Figure 11-21.** Be sure there are no sharp ends that might catch at conduit joints. Pull wires through conduit. Using wire-pulling lubricant will help make pulling of the wires easier.

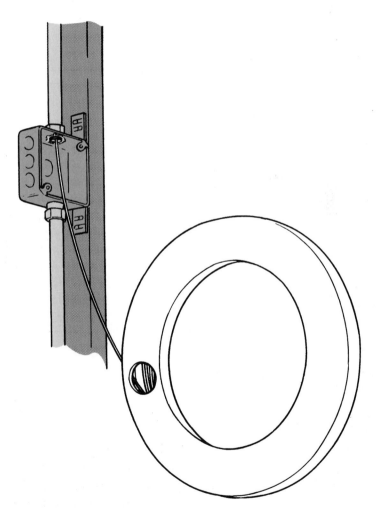

Figure 11-20. Using fish tape.

Figure 11-21. End of fish tape showing loop and how wires are fastened to the tape.

One type of wire lubricant comes in an aerosol can. The material is dispensed into the end of the conduit as a creamy foam. The lubricant clings to the wires as they are pulled into the conduit. Wire-pulling lubricants also come in liquid and paste forms.

Circuit Breakers and Fuses

Circuit breakers and *fuses* act as *safety valves* for the wiring system. They protect the wiring from overloads and short circuits.

Circuit breakers

The circuit breaker is the type of overcurrent device most frequently used today. Breakers are safe, reliable, and easy to use. This accounts for their popularity.

A single-pole circuit breaker of the thermal magnetic type is shown in **Figure 11-22**. This breaker has a bimetallic element, which consists of two strips of dissimilar metals bonded together. This bimetallic element responds to changes in temperature within the circuit. When excessive current, or overcurrent, is flowing through the circuit, the heat created by the resistance on the bimetallic unit expands each metal at a different rate. The different rates of expansion cause the strip to bend and open the circuit. This is what is referred to as *tripping the circuit breaker.*

Individual circuit breakers are rated in amperes and come in a variety of sizes and rating capabilities. See **Figure 11-23**. They carry their load continuously, and can overload for short periods of time, as required to start motors, air conditioners, clothes dryers, etc.

The *circuit breaker panel box* contains the main breaker, 240-volt circuits, and/or 120- volt circuits. See **Figure 11-24**. The *main breaker* connects all current to the circuit. The circuit breaker panel should be located as close to the incoming service as possible. It should have a capacity sufficient to supply present and future demands.

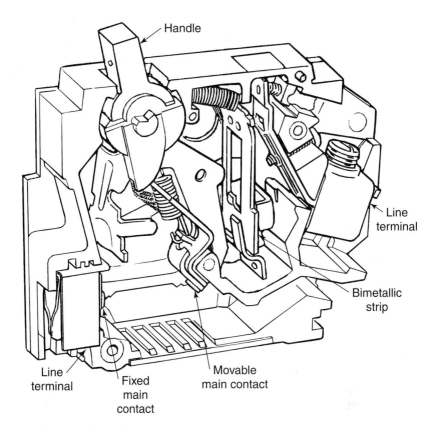

Figure 11-22. A circuit breaker is a switch in the black or hot wire that opens automatically when a predetermined current overload flows through it. Individual breakers are grouped and placed in an entrance panel box. Each individual circuit requires a separate breaker. (General Electric)

Fuses

An entrance panel that makes use of fuses instead of circuit breakers to protect against shorts and overloads of the circuits is shown in **Figure 11-25.** The fuses screw in and out like lightbulbs.

In a standard plug-type fuse, as shown in **Figure 11-26,** the current passes through the metal strip running across the face of the fuse. When the fuse is blown by overloading, the metal strip overheats and melts at the weakest point. This breaks the flow of current. When a fuse is blown because of overloading, the fuse window

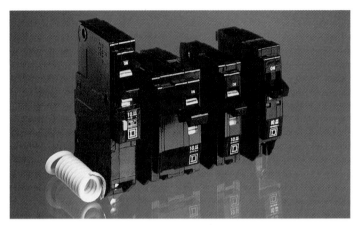

Figure 11-23. Circuit breakers come in a variety of sizes and capabilities. (Square D Co.)

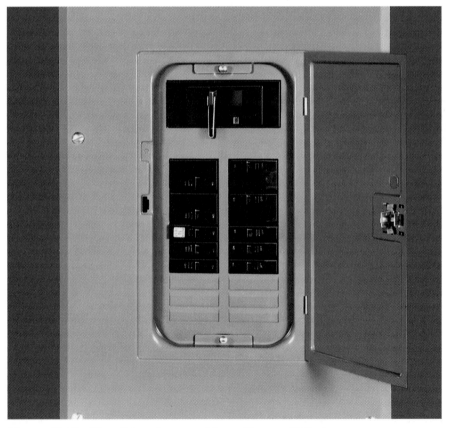

Figure 11-24. Circuit breaker panel box. (Square D Co.)

Figure 11-25. Entrance panel—100 amps., 240 volts, with 8 branch circuits.

Figure 11-26. Plug-type fuse. The glass top helps prevent shocks when changing fuses.

remains clear. If the fuse is blown because of a short circuit, the metal strip is heated to a high temperature and vaporizes. This discolors the fuse window. See **Figure 11-27.**

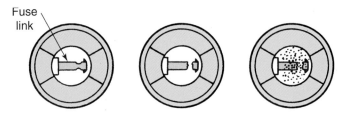

Figure 11-27. Plug-type fuses. Left. New fuse. Current passes through strip of thin metal (fuse link). Center. Fuse blown by overload. Right. Fuse blown by short circuit.

Plug-type fuses are made in capacities up to 30 amperes. Where No. 14 wire is used, 15 ampere fuses are the largest that may be used; 20 ampere fuses are the largest that may be used with No. 12 wire. Cartridge-type fuses, as used in house wiring, come in capacities up to 100 amperes, **Figure 11-28.**

Figure 11-28. Cartridge-type fuses.

Fustats, **Figures 11-29** and **11-30,** are tamper-resistant protective devices that provide delayed fuse action. When a short circuit develops, the fuse link blows the same as in a regular fuse. For moderate overloads, instead of the fuse link blowing, the solder cup starts to heat. If the overload continues, the solder in the cup softens, and the spring pulls the fuse link out of the solder cup, opening the circuit.

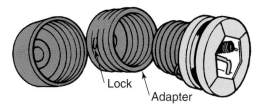

Figure 11-29. Fustat and adapter.

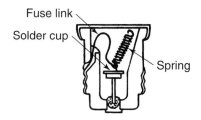

Figure 11-30. How fustat is constructed.

With each different size of fustat (15 amps., 20 amps., etc.), a different fustat adapter is required. The adapter is constructed so when it is screwed into the socket it locks in place. It cannot readily be removed. This prevents inserting fuses that are too large.

In addition to fustats, time-delay plug fuses are available. These fuses are used with circuits that can draw very high currents during a startup condition. Circuits that supply current to devices with large motors are candidates for protection with time-delay fuses.

Also available for protecting electrical wiring circuit are miniature circuit breakers that screw into ordinary fuse sockets, **Figure 11-31.** The protector trips on dangerous overloads or short circuits. Service is restored by pressing a small button that protrudes from the top.

Figure 11-31. Small circuit breaker that screws into fuse socket.

Caution: **When a fuse is blown, open the main switch or pull out the section of the panel labeled "main" to cut off the current. Correct the condition that caused the overload, then replace the blown fuse with a new one of the proper size. Make sure your hands are dry, and stand on a dry board. Close the main switch or replace the pull-out section of the panel to restore service.**

Additional Information

The reference section of this book contains a number of useful tables quoted from the *National Electrical Code.* See pages 149 to 180.

Review Questions

Please do not write in the text. Place your answers on a separate sheet of paper.

1. To identify the conductors in a house wiring system, the wires are _____ coded.
2. *True or False?* The *National Electrical Code* requires that the neutral or ground wire to be white and the hot wire to be a color, such as black, red, green, or blue.
3. A white wire is actually a current-carrying _____ for the 120-volt circuit.
4. Connecting the two colored wires and the white wire in a 3-wire circuit provides _____ volts.
5. When connecting wires to terminals, black wires should be connected to _____ colored terminals on outlet receptacles and the white wires should be connected to the _____ colored terminals.
6. *True or False?* Switches are always connected to one white wire and one black wire.
7. All solderless connections must be enclosed in _____ _____.
8. Connecting one end of a wire to a point on a continuous wire is called a(n) _____ splice.
9. Wire-pulling lubricant comes in the form of:
   a. creamy foam.
   b. liquid.
   c. paste.
   d. All of the above.
10. Circuit breakers and fuses protect wiring systems from _____ and _____ circuits.
11. When a fuse blows because of a(n) _____, the fuse window remains clear.
12. After a fuse has blown and the trouble is corrected, replace the blown fuse with one of the _____ size.

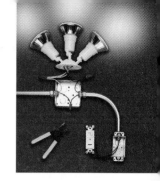

Unit 12
House Wiring
Circuits

In this unit, easy-to-understand drawings show how to install wiring required for switches, outlets, and fixtures. While the drawings show only conduit being used, you may be able to substitute BX or Romex. Be sure to check your local electrical code.

Figure 12-1. To add a switch, cut the black wire and attach both ends to the terminal screws of the switch. Run the conduit ends into a new box. Use a solderless connector to connect the two white wires.

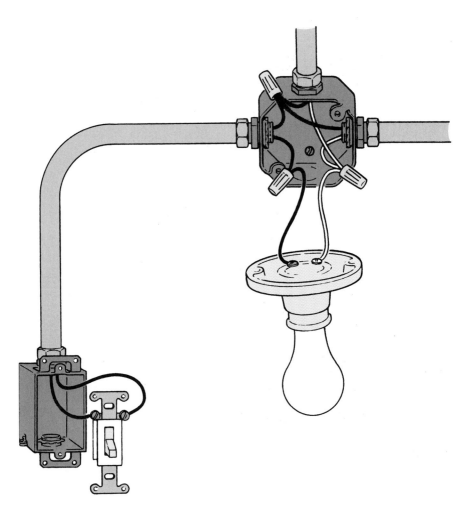

Figure 12-2. Using a wall switch to control light away from the switch. Note that all wiring to the switch is black wire. If nonmetallic or armored cable is used in wiring instead of conduit, a 2-wire cable (one white wire, one black wire) may be used. This special use of a white wire as a hot wire is approved by the code. Both ends of the white wire should be painted black. While the conduit itself provides sufficient ground, a grounding wire is required with BX, nonmetallic cable, and plastic conduit.

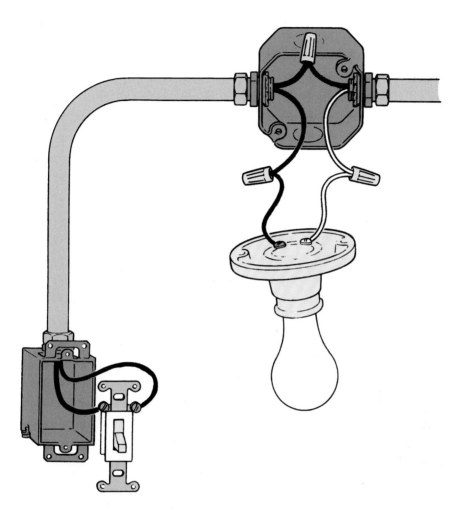

Figure 12-3. Installing wall switch to control light at end of run.

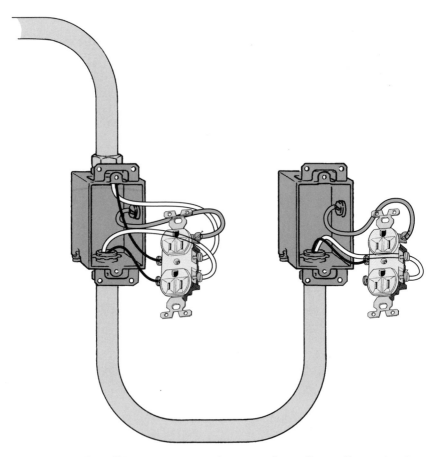

Figure 12-4. Installing two convenience outlets. Grounding wire is not necessary with metal conduit but is required with other conductor systems. Note the positioning of the grounding terminal. It is good practice to position the grounding terminals on top when installing outlets. It can help prevent a short circuit if a metal object is dropped onto the plug.

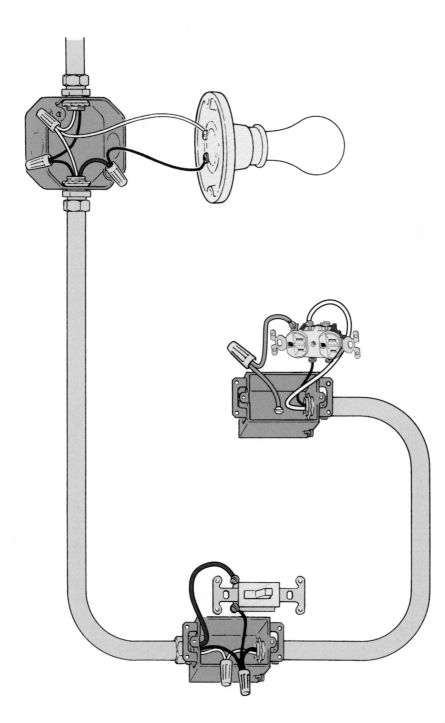

Figure 12-5. Installing the outlet and switch beyond a light. The switch controls the light; the outlet is always hot.

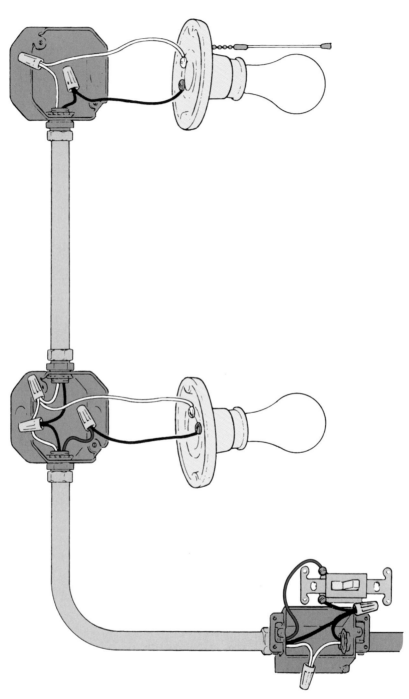

Figure 12-6. Two ceiling lights on the same line. One is controlled with a wall switch, the other is controlled with a pull chain switch.

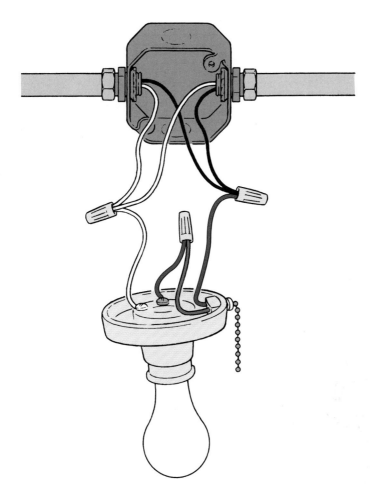

Figure 12-7. Light controlled by a canopy switch.

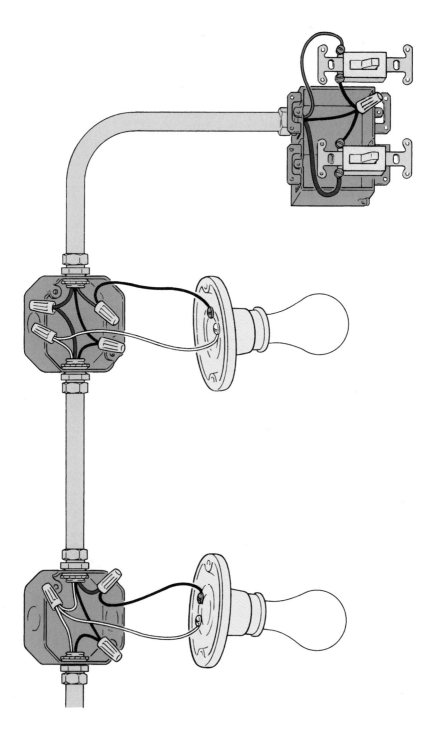

Figure 12-8. Two ceiling lights operated by individual switches.

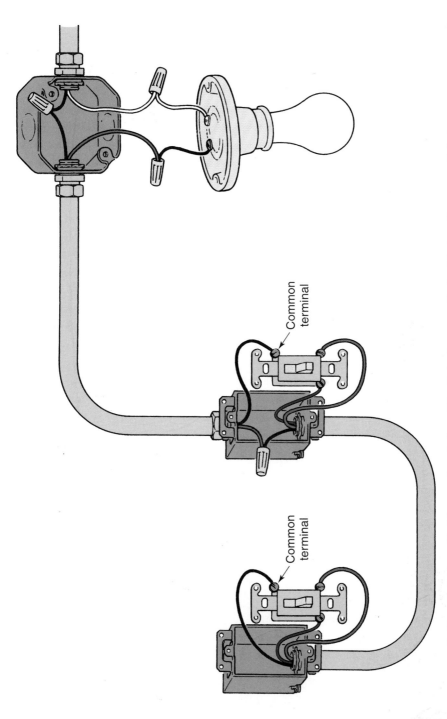

Figure 12-9. Ceiling light installed beyond switches. The light is controlled with two 3-way switches.

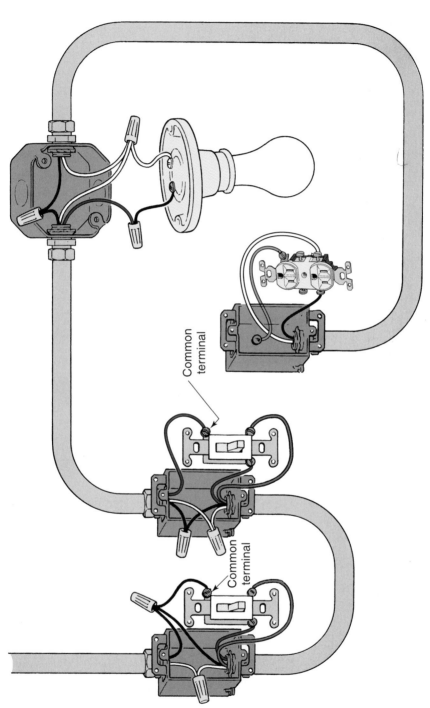

Common terminal

Common terminal

Figure 12-10. Ceiling light and receptacle installed beyond two 3-way switches. The receptacle is always hot. Note: Grounding of ceramic fixtures is not required by code but is required with other types of fixtures.

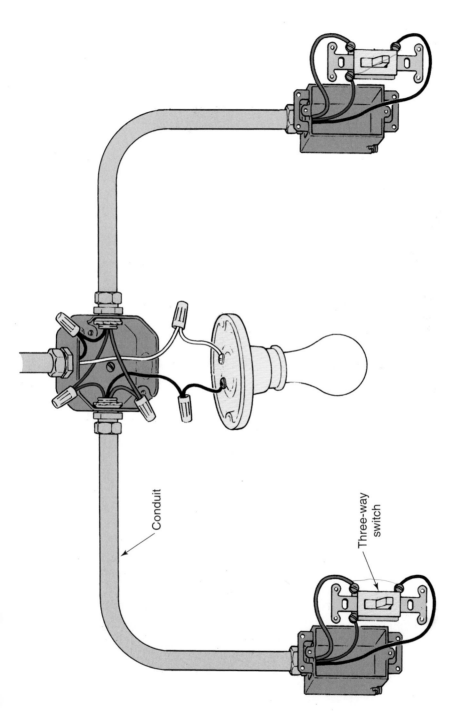

Conduit

Three-way switch

Figure 12-11. Ceiling light with two 3-way switches.

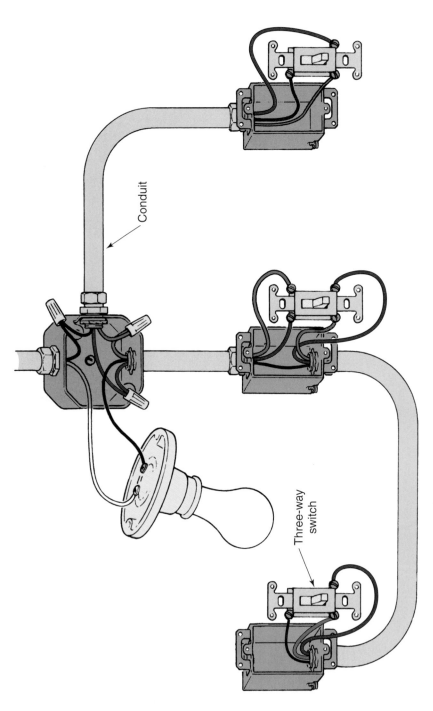

Conduit

Three-way switch

Figure 12-12. Installing 4-way switch with two 3-way switches to control a light fixture from three points.

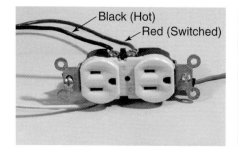

Black (Hot)
Red (Switched)

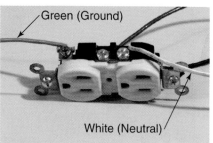

Green (Ground)

White (Neutral)

Break tab to
separate circuits

Figure 12-13. Split circuit wiring provides two separate circuits at each outlet receptacle. This may be used where there are two or more heavy appliances and each outlet must be on a separate circuit breaker. Another situation, which is more likely, requires a split circuit installation to accommodate a switched outlet. One outlet is continuously hot while the other is controlled by a wall switch. This allows a lamp to be plugged into the outlet and controlled by the wall switch. The other outlet may be used by a clock or other appliance that would require continuous power.

To create the split circuit, remove the metal tab that is located between the two brass-colored screws. Do not remove the tab between the silver-colored screws, unless a separate neutral wire will be attached to each screw. The tab is removed by bending it with a screwdriver or pliers, depending on the style of the tab. See the manufacturer's instructions for more information.

Once the tab is removed, attach the hot wire to one brass-colored screw, the switched wire to the other brass-colored screw, the white (neutral) wire to one of the silver-colored screws, and the green (ground) wire to the ground screw.

Entrance panel

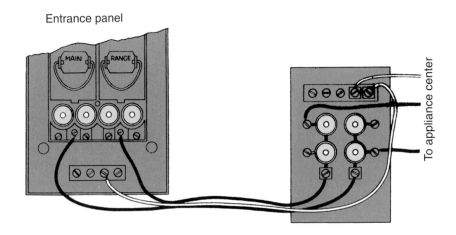

Figure 12-14. Installing fuse or circuit breaker panel to provide new circuits, when there are no unused circuits on entrance panel. Connect two black wires to power take-off lugs and white wire to neutral strip of service entrance panel. This provides 120 volts between the black and white wires and 240 volts between the two black wires. Open wires are shown between panels for clarity. Wiring must meet codes.

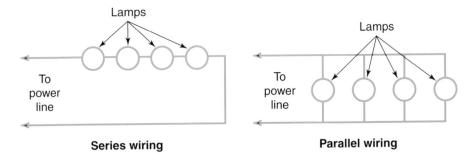

Figure 12-15. Series and parallel circuits. In *series* circuits, to operate the first lamp electricity must pass through all of the lamps. Series wiring is sometimes used when it is desirable to operate several low-voltage lamps (like Christmas tree lights) on a line of higher voltage. With *parallel* circuits, each lamp can be operated individually.

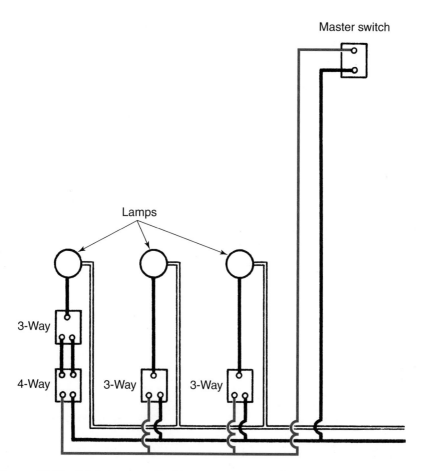

Figure 12-16. Wiring controlled by a master switch.

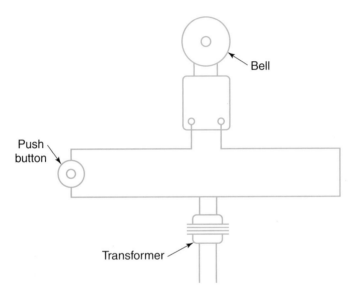

Figure 12-17. A simple, transformer-operated signal system. No. 18 bell wire is ordinarily used to make the hookup from the transformer to the bell. (See the *National Electric Code* concerning use of bell wire.)

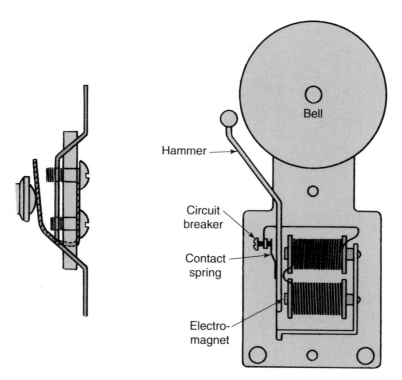

Figure 12-18. Left. Push-button switch. Pressure against button causes a movable contact to meet a fixed contact and close circuit. Right. Doorbell with principal parts identified.

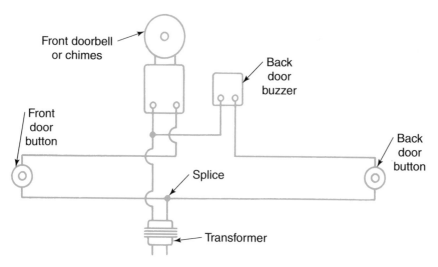

Figure 12-19. Wiring diagram for front and back entrances, using both a bell and buzzer.

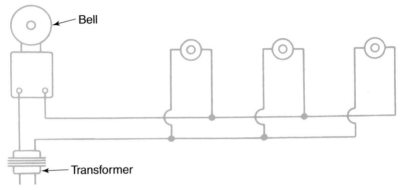

Figure 12-20. Diagram showing one bell controlled from three places.

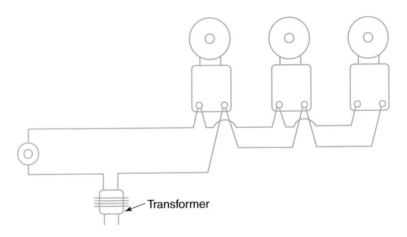

Figure 12-21. Three bells controlled by one push-button switch.

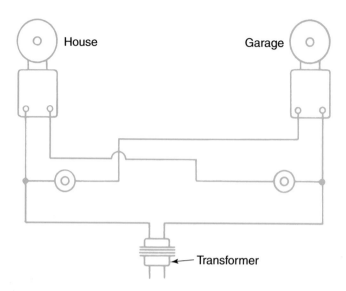

Figure 12-22. Hookup for 3-wire return signal system.

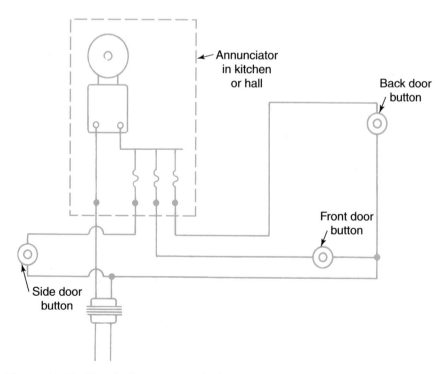

Figure 12-23. Doorbell system with three stations.

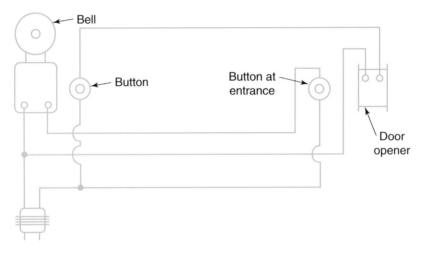

Figure 12-24. Bell and door opener circuit.

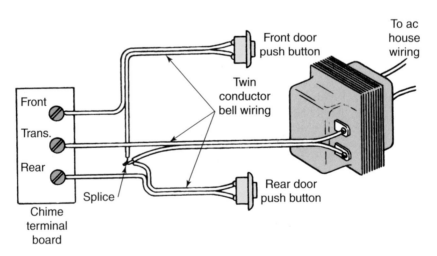

Figure 12-25. Wiring for two-note (NuTone) chime.

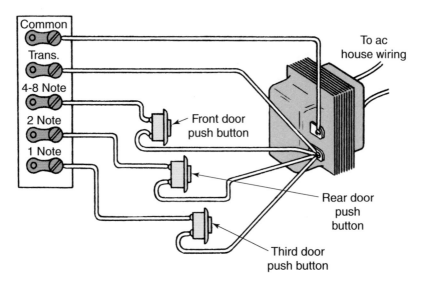

Figure 12-26. Wiring for eight-note chime.

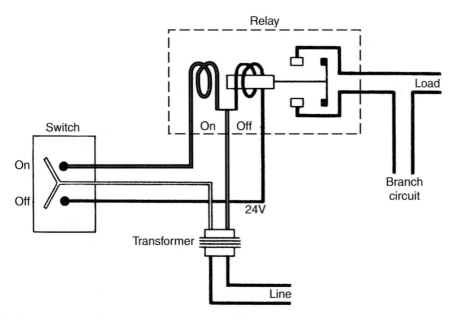

Figure 12-27. Basic circuit for General Electric's remote-control, low-voltage switching system. Relays handle the switching of the current. The relays are controlled by switches operating at low voltage that permit the use of wiring similar to that used for door chimes. Many different components are available. In planning and installing remote control systems, follow instructions supplied by the manufacturer of the equipment.

Selection of styles for low-voltage outdoor lighting.
(LT-Licht Technik GmbH)

Unit 13
Modernizing
Electrical Systems

Installing electrical wiring in a home while it is being constructed is called **new work.** Providing wiring needed to install switches, outlets, and fixtures in a home that is already built is called **old work.**

In both new work and old work, the same basic wiring principles are involved.

Wiring in new work is largely a matter of mounting metal boxes on the framework and running the conduit or cables to those boxes, following the most direct route. When conduit is used, the wires are fished through the conduit and the necessary connections made after the walls are completed.

Old work, where the wires are to be concealed, involves getting cables and wires from one point to another with the least effort and minimum damage to structural members and finished walls.

Armored (BX) cable, plastic cable, and nonmetallic sheathed cable are used extensively for old concealed wiring, because they are flexible and can be pulled through openings between walls, ceilings, and floors easily. The *National Electrical Code* prohibits running flexible cord through holes in walls, ceilings, floors, etc. and using it as a substitute for cable.

Old work frequently requires more material than new work. It is easier to run the cable through channels that are readily accessible rather than tear up ceilings, floors, and walls.

Solving problems that arise obviously requires some ingenuity on the part of the electrician handling the job.

Check Codes

In doing a job of modernizing a wiring system, check the requirements of the local building codes and ordinances and see that all requirements are met. It would also be well to obtain a copy of the *National Electrical Code* and have it available for ready reference.

Safety: **Be sure the electricity is disconnected before disconnecting any wires or making wiring hookups. Don't take chances.**

Installing New Outlets

First decide where the new outlets are to be located, then figure out the best way to run cables to them. One end of the new cable must be run to an existing outlet box that contains a black wire (hot) and a ground wire (white) and is not already overloaded with circuits. See **Figures 13-1** and **13-2.** Another possibility is to bring power from the entrance panel and start a new circuit.

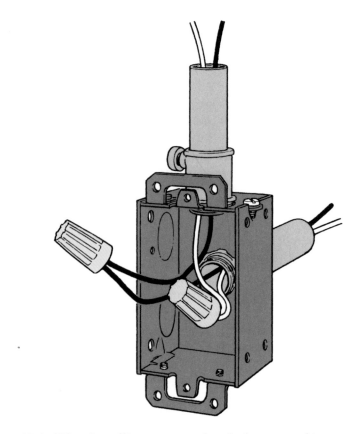

Figure 13-1. When installing a new outlet, the box tapped into must contain a black wire (which is continuously live), a white wire, and it must not be overloaded with circuits.

Box dimensions, inches Trade size	Maximum number of conductors for boxes			
	No. 14	No. 12	No. 10	No. 8
4 × 1 1/4 and or Octagonal	6	5	5	4
4 × 1 1/2 and or Octagonal	7	6	6	5
4 × 2 1/8 and or Octagonal	10	9	8	7
4 × 1 1/4 Square	9	8	7	6
4 × 1 1/2 Square	10	9	8	7
4 × 2 1/8 Square	15	13	12	10
4 11/16 × 1 1/4 Square	12	11	10	8
4 11/16 × 1 1/2 Square	14	13	11	9
4 11/16 × 2 1/8 Square	21	18	16	14
3 × 2 × 1 1/2 Rectangular	3	3	3	2
3 × 2 × 2 Rectangular	5	4	4	3
3 × 2 × 2 1/4 Rectangular	5	4	4	3
3 × 2 × 2 1/2 Rectangular	6	5	5	4
3 × 2 × 2 3/4 Rectangular	7	6	5	4
3 × 2 × 3 1/2 Rectangular	9	8	7	6
4 × 2 1/8 × 1 1/2 Rectangular	5	4	4	3
4 × 2 1/8 × 1 7/8 Rectangular	6	5	5	4
4 × 2 1/8 × 2 1/8 Rectangular	7	6	5	5

Figure 13-2. Maximum number of conductors that can be used in boxes.

Keep in mind the fact that all wire splices must be enclosed in boxes, and that each switch and convenience outlet must be housed in a box. Each fixture must be attached to a box.

In old work, rectangular boxes are generally used because they are relatively easy to install with minimum marring of the walls.

In old wiring, where the system is grounded back to the entrance service panel (this is usually the case where conduit or armored cable has been used), outlet receptacles of the grounding type must be used. These have a U-shaped opening for the prong on a 3-wire plug and a green colored grounding terminal, **Figure 13-3.** A grounding wire must be run from the green terminal of the receptacle to the box.

The wire can be fastened to the box using a sheet metal screw inserted in a hole provided for the purpose or with a metal clip, **Figure 13-4.**

Figure 13-3. A 20 amp outlet receptacle with a U-shaped opening and a grounding terminal.

Figure 13-4. Two ways of connecting the grounding wire to a metal box.

Back-to-back outlets

Figure 13-5 shows how a new outlet can be installed in the wall in back of an existing outlet.

Decide on a location for the box. Measure from door opening and baseboard. Drill a small hole (1/16 in.) through the wall. Use a piece of wire as a probe to make sure there are no obstructions that will interfere with the installation.

Use a template for wall marking as shown in **Figures 13-6** and **13-7.**

If the wall is lath and plaster or of other material that will not hold nails, an outlet box of the type that has screw-type clamps on

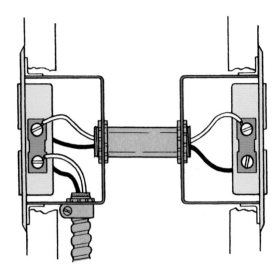

Figure 13-5. Installing a new outlet in wall in back of an old outlet.

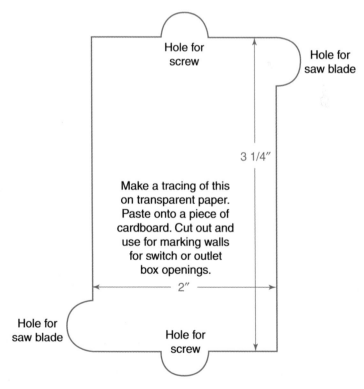

Hole for screw

Hole for saw blade

3 1/4″

Make a tracing of this on transparent paper. Paste onto a piece of cardboard. Cut out and use for marking walls for switch or outlet box openings.

2″

Hole for saw blade

Hole for screw

Figure 13-6. Full-size template for marking wall area opening to take an outlet box.

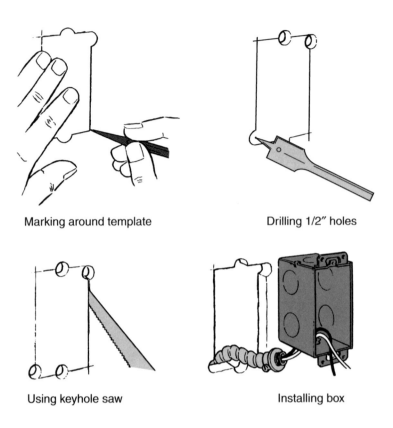

Marking around template   Drilling 1/2" holes

Using keyhole saw   Installing box

Figure 13-7. Preparing a wall opening for an outlet box.

the side can be used. See **Figure 13-8.** Or, you can use metal supports to hold a box of standard type, **Figure 13-9.**

If the wall is lath and plaster, chip away plaster to determine lath locations. Then, cut one full lath and notch the top and bottom laths, **Figure 13-10.**

Installing new outlets from a wall switch

Figure 13-11 shows how to run a cable from a wall switch (provided a neutral ground white wire is available) to new outlet installed above the baseboard. Remove the baseboard, chip plaster, or cut drywall to make channel for BX cable as indicated. All bends must be made so the cable is not injured. The radius of the inner edge should not be less than five times the diameter of the cable. No splices in the cable are permitted between boxes.

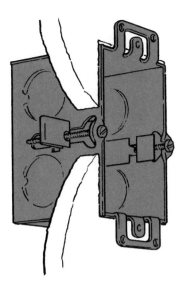

Figure 13-8. Installing a box with side brackets in drywall. Side screws are tightened to bring the brackets against the wall and hold the box in place.

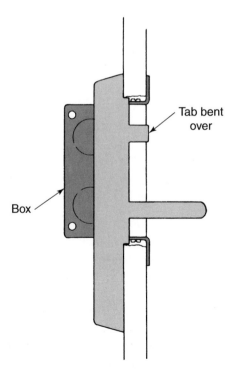

Figure 13-9. Using metal supports to hold the box in place.

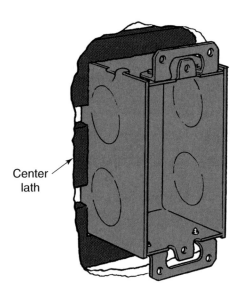

Center
lath

Figure 13-10. Cut through center lath, and notch laths above and below.

If you have a job of installing an outlet on the first floor, you can run the BX cable across the basement. Proceed as shown in **Figures 13-12** and **13-13.** Use a long-shank bit to bore a hole at an angle.

Basement light to first floor outlet

Figure 13-14 illustrates the procedure used to follow in running a cable from a basement light (with switch at light and ground wire in box) to a new outlet.

Running Cable Around a Door

To run a cable around a door and install an outlet on the other side of the door, refer to **Figure 13-15.** Remove the door trim and a section of baseboard. Notch spacers to take BX cable. Run the cable, then replace door trim and baseboard.

Installing a Wall Switch

Installing a wall switch for a ceiling light that has been controlled previously by a pull switch at the fixture is shown in **Figure 13-16.** A 2-wire cable (one black wire, one white) is run from the light to the box in which the new switch is to be installed. Be sure to mark both

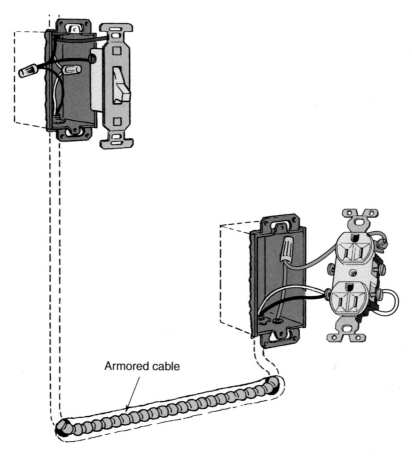

Figure 13-11. Running cable from a wall switch to a new outlet above baseboard.

ends of the white wire with black paint so others will know both wires are hot. Connecting a black wire to a white wire is permitted by the Code if cable is used (not permitted when using conduit).

Fishing Cable Through a Wall

Fishing a cable from the attic or room above the new installation is shown in **Figure 13-17.** Remove baseboard and drill a hole diagonally downward as indicated in the top drawing. Push fish wires with hooks at the ends through the opening. Withdraw one wire until it hooks the other (lower drawing, Figure 13-17), then withdraw second wire until hooks meet. Attach to the wires in the BX cable and pull cable through the opening.

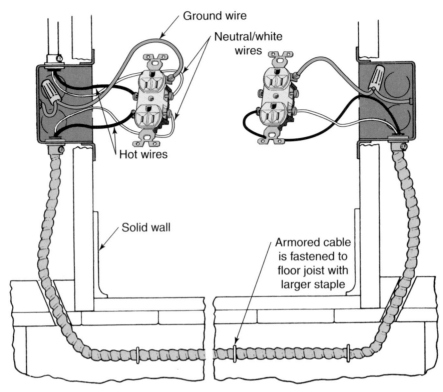

Figure 13-12. Installing an outlet by running cable through the floor and across the basement.

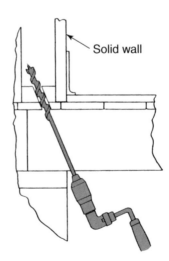

Figure 13-13. Boring hole diagonally from basement through the floor so that cable can be run between walls.

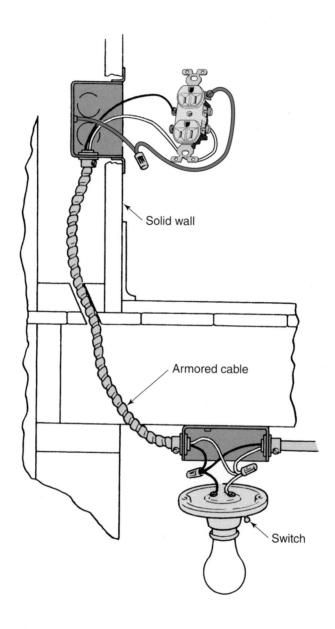

Figure 13-14. Running cable from a basement light to a new outlet on first floor.

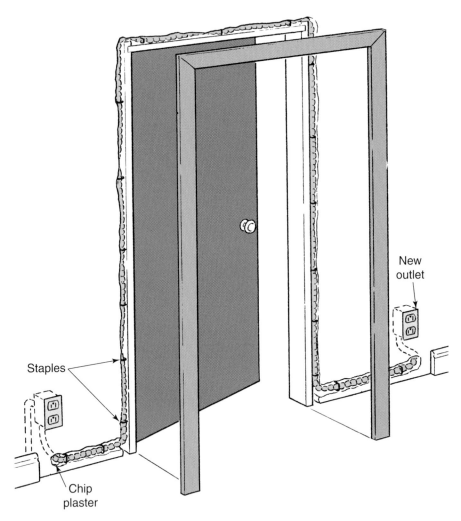

New
outlet

Staples

Chip
plaster

Figure 13-15. Running cable around a door to install an outlet on the other side.

Lifting Attic Floorboards

The drawings, **Figures 13-18** and **13-19,** show lifting attic floorboards and drilling the joists to take a cable. See where the joist is nailed. Then bore small holes (1/16 in.) to locate the edge of the joist. If the flooring is of the tongue-and-groove type, you can use a floor chisel or putty knife with the edge sharpened and a hammer to cut through the tongue on both sides of the portion to be removed. Bore holes at the corners large enough to take a small keyhole saw blade,

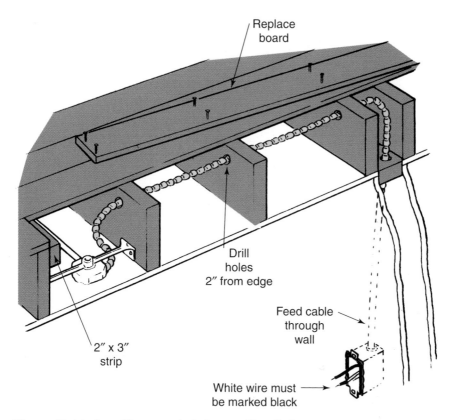

Replace board

Drill holes 2" from edge

Feed cable through wall

2" x 3" strip

White wire must be marked black

Figure 13-16. Installing a switch for a ceiling light.

and saw through the board in two places. Drill a hole in the joists to take the cable, **Figure 13-19,** and nail a cleat to the joists to support the floorboard when it is replaced, Figure 13-18.

Installing an octagon box is shown in **Figure 13-20.** In old work where it is impractical to install an octagon shaped box of regular depth, a shallow round box and an old work hanger, can be used, **Figure 13-21.** Round boxes must not be used where conduits or connectors requiring the use of locknuts or where bushings are to be connected to the side of the box.

Surface Wiring

In modernizing house wiring, the use of some surface wiring devices in inconspicuous areas, which can be a real timesaver, should be considered. See **Figure 13-22.**

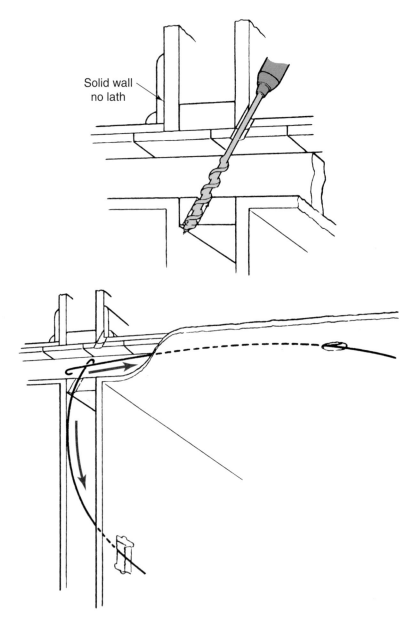

Figure 13-17. Fishing cable through the wall from the room above.

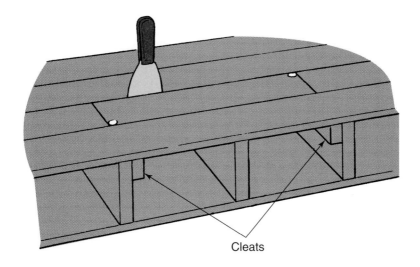

Cleats

Figure 13-18. Preparing a section of an attic floorboard for removal.

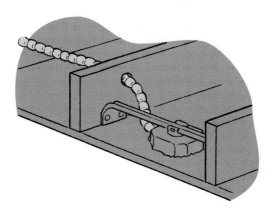

Figure 13-19. Attic floor joists are drilled to take cable.

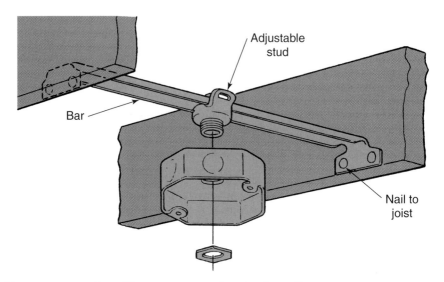

Figure 13-20.   Installing an octagon box in the ceiling.

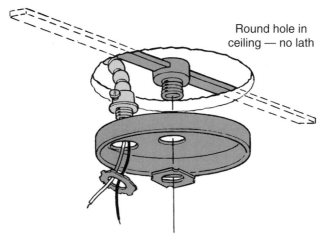

Figure 13-21. Old work. Installing shallow, round box using special old work hanger.

Outdoor Wiring

Installing a yard light (typical installation) is shown in **Figure 13-23.** The light is switch controlled from the house. The control can be manual or automatic by a time switch. The convenience outlets are

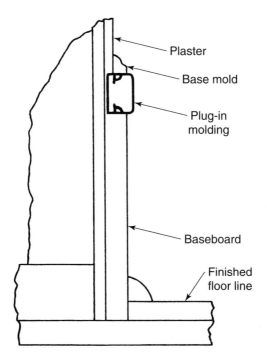

Figure 13-22. Using surface mounted plug-in molding.

always on. An easy way to provide the necessary wiring from the house to the light is to use dual-purpose plastic cable (referred to as type UF Direct Burial). Check local codes. It may be that the cable must be encased in conduit. Keep in mind that the principles involved in outdoor wiring and indoor wiring are basically the same.

Low voltage equipment

Typical low voltage (6 to 12 volts) lighting equipment designed for outdoor use is shown in **Figure 13-24.** This is used in connection with regular 120 volt equipment. Low voltage lighting is ideal for lighting small gardens and for providing specific accents in larger gardens.

Winter roof drainage

Using electric heating cable to prevent downspout and gutter freezeup is shown in **Figure 13-25.** Lay cable in roof gutters, drop end in downspout, and then fasten cable to roof with special clips provided. Electricity required can be provided by installing an outdoor type outlet box or by using a heavy-duty extension cord run from a nearby outdoor outlet.

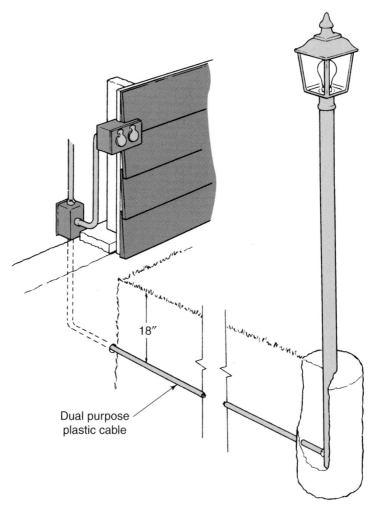

18″

Dual purpose plastic cable

Figure 13-23. Outdoor wiring. Installing outlets and light.

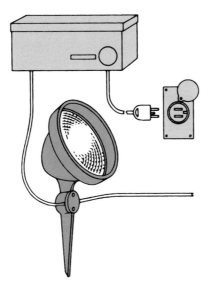

Figure 13-24.   Low-voltage wiring for outdoor use.

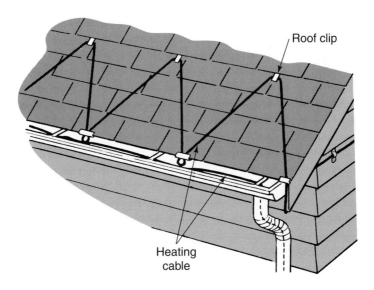

Figure 13-25.   Using heating cable to prevent gutter and downspout freezeup.

Review Questions

Please do not write in the text. Place your answers on a separate sheet of paper.

1. *True or False?* Different basic wiring principles are involved in wiring new work and in wiring old work.
2. Three kinds of cable used extensively for old concealed wiring are:
   a. _____
   b. _____
   c. _____
3. When installing new outlets, one end of the new cable must run to an existing outlet box that contains a(n) _____ wire and a(n) _____ wire and is not _____.
4. What type of outlet receptacles must be used in old wiring where the system is grounded back to the entrance service panel?
5. For marking wall openings to take boxes, use a(n) _____ of the same size.
6. When bending BX cable, the radius of the inner edge should not be less than _____ times the diameter of the cable.
7. In modernizing, when a 2-wire cable is run from a light to a box in which a new switch is to be installed, be sure to mark both ends of the wire so others will know it is _____.

Unit 14
Useful Information

Extension Cords

Extension cords are used to reach outlets that are not close enough to plug appliances into directly. These cords are made up of fine strands of copper, so they will be flexible. Each cord has a maximum allowable current-carrying capacity, **Figure 14-1.** Appliances and power tools that have grounding plugs should be used only with 3-wire grounding type extension cords and plugged into 3-hole grounding outlets.

Ability of Cord to Carry Current (2- or 3-Wire Cord)		
Wire size	Normal load	Capacity load
No. 18	5.0 Amp. (600W)	7 Amp. (840W)
No. 16	8.3 Amp. (1000W)	10 Amp. (1200W)
No. 14	12.5 Amp. (1500 W)	15 Amp. (1800W)
No. 12	16.6 Amp. (1900W)	20 Amp. (2400W)

	Wire size	Use
Ordinary lamp cord	No. 16 or 18	In residences for lamps or small appliances.
Heavy-duty – with thicker covering	No. 10, 12, 14, or 16	In shops, and outdoors for larger motors, lawn mowers, outdoor lighting, etc.

Selecting Length of Cord		
Light load (to 7 amps.)	Medium load (7-10 amps.)	Heavy load (10-15 amps.)
To 25 Ft. – Use No. 18	To 25 Ft. – Use No. 16	To 25 Ft. – Use No. 14
To 50 Ft. – Use No. 16	To 50 Ft. – Use No. 14	To 50 Ft. – Use No. 12
To 100 Ft. – Use No. 14	To 100 Ft. – Use No. 12	To 100 Ft. – Use No. 10

Figure 14-1. Selecting the proper type of extension cord for the job at hand.

Damaged or frayed cords provide serious fire hazards and should be replaced. Exception: A cord that is frayed only at one end can sometimes be repaired. Cut the cord to remove the damaged portion. Then attach the wire ends to a new plug.

Reading Electric Meters

Electric meters register in kilowatt-hour units. A kilowatt-hour is 1000 watts in operation for one hour.

Figure 14-2 shows how the four dials look on a typical meter. Arrows indicate the directions the hands rotate.

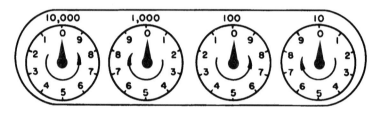

Figure 14-2. Dials of a typical electric meter. The arrows indicate the direction hands on the dials rotate.

To take a reading, you must read all four dials of the meter. The figures on the dial at the extreme right measure individual kilowatt-hours. Each figure on the second dial from the right shows 10 kilowatt-hours. Each figure on the third dial from the right represents 100 kilowatt-hours. Each figure on the dial at the left represents 1000 kilowatt-hours.

To fix these values in your mind, remember that the dial at the extreme right is capable of registering 10 kilowatt-hours. The second dial from the right is capable of registering 100 kilowatt-hours. The third dial from the right is capable of registering 1000 kilowatt-hours. The dial at the left will register 10,000 kilowatt-hours.

In each case, the last figure passed by the hand, and not the nearest, is used in the reading. When the hand seems to be right on the number, the dial to the right of the dial being read should be consulted to see whether or not the number has been passed.

In reading a meter, always start with the dial on the right and remember that the pointer on the right dial must make one complete revolution before the indicator on the next dial moves one number.

The kilowatt-hours used in a month are determined by subtracting the reading at the start of the month from the end-of-the-month reading. Before you can figure the cost of the electrical energy used, you must obtain information on rates from the utility company. You will find that the cost per kilowatt-hour goes down as you use more electricity.

LightBulbs

Lightbulbs come in a variety of shapes, sizes, wattages, and types. The two most common types of bulbs found in the home are incandescent and fluorescent.

Incandescent lamps

Incandescent bulbs, though not as energy efficient as fluorescent bulbs, are the most common type found in house lighting. Their low cost and small size make them convenient. **Figure 14-3** shows the structure of a typical incandescent bulb.

Three-way incandescent bulbs, **Figure 14-4,** use two filaments to provide three different light intensities.

Figure 14-5 shows numerous shapes for incandescent bulbs. They all provide different lighting effects. **Figure 14-6** shows the structure of a mercury lightbulb.

Incandescent bulbs are often used in simple test lights. **Figure 14-7** shows a test light you can make yourself.

Fluorescent lamps

The fluorescent lamp, **Figure 14-8,** is usually a long narrow or circular glass cylinder, coated on the interior with any of several types of phosphor (chemical coating that will radiate light). Air in the tube is replaced with mercury vapor and argon, an inert (chemically inactive) gas. At each end of the lamp is an electrode, made of an oxide-coated tungsten filament. When heated by an electric current, the filament releases a cloud of electrons around each electrode.

A high voltage electrical surge then establishes an electron arc between the electrodes with each alternation of the current. The electrons collide with mercury vapor and argon gas atoms filling the tube to produce invisible ultraviolet rays.

The rays excite the fluorescent phosphor coating the inside of the tube to become visible light.

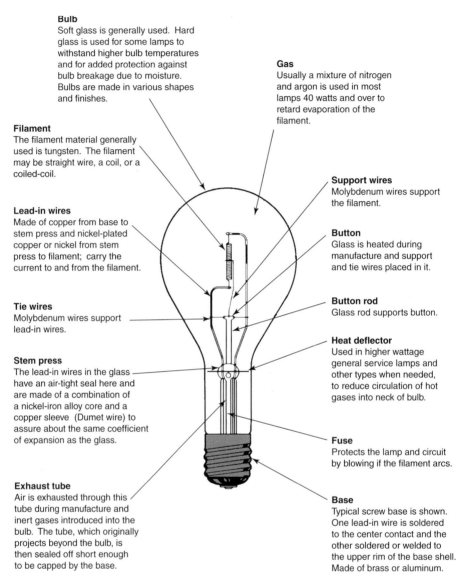

Bulb
Soft glass is generally used. Hard glass is used for some lamps to withstand higher bulb temperatures and for added protection against bulb breakage due to moisture. Bulbs are made in various shapes and finishes.

Gas
Usually a mixture of nitrogen and argon is used in most lamps 40 watts and over to retard evaporation of the filament.

Filament
The filament material generally used is tungsten. The filament may be straight wire, a coil, or a coiled-coil.

Lead-in wires
Made of copper from base to stem press and nickel-plated copper or nickel from stem press to filament; carry the current to and from the filament.

Support wires
Molybdenum wires support the filament.

Button
Glass is heated during manufacture and support and tie wires placed in it.

Tie wires
Molybdenum wires support lead-in wires.

Button rod
Glass rod supports button.

Stem press
The lead-in wires in the glass have an air-tight seal here and are made of a combination of a nickel-iron alloy core and a copper sleeve (Dumet wire) to assure about the same coefficient of expansion as the glass.

Heat deflector
Used in higher wattage general service lamps and other types when needed, to reduce circulation of hot gases into neck of bulb.

Fuse
Protects the lamp and circuit by blowing if the filament arcs.

Exhaust tube
Air is exhausted through this tube during manufacture and inert gases introduced into the bulb. The tube, which originally projects beyond the bulb, is then sealed off short enough to be capped by the base.

Base
Typical screw base is shown. One lead-in wire is soldered to the center contact and the other soldered or welded to the upper rim of the base shell. Made of brass or aluminum.

Figure 14-3. Typical incandescent lamp bulb. This type produces a high lighting level over a relatively long period of time. Longer lasting lamps can be produced but the light output is lower. Additional light is produced at the expense of lamp life. Modern incandescent lamps strike a balance between light intensity and lamp life. Bulb blackening is the result of depositing of tungsten particles on inner surface of the bulb. (Sylvania)

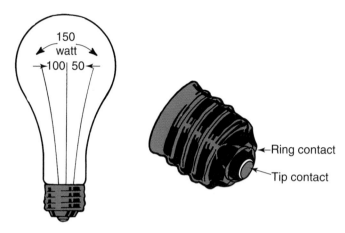

Figure 14-4. Typical 3-way bulbs have two filaments. Each filament can be operated separately, or in combination with the other. First, the low-wattage filament is switched on, next the high-wattage filament, then the two are switched on together. A special 3-way socket with two contacts in the base, and a 3-way switch are required. (General Electric)

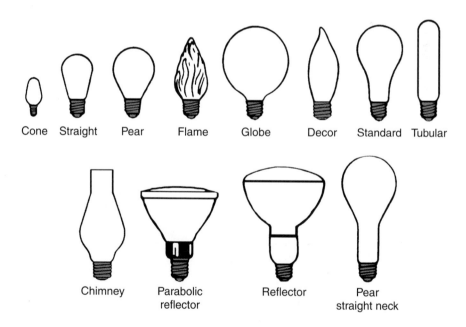

Figure 14-5. Incandescent lamp bulb shapes.

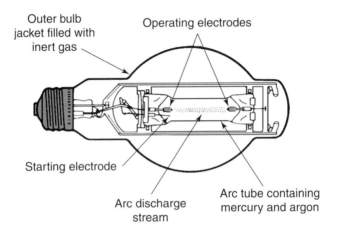

Outer bulb jacket filled with inert gas

Operating electrodes

Starting electrode

Arc discharge stream

Arc tube containing mercury and argon

Figure 14-6. Mercury lamp that produces light by passing an alternating current through mercury vapor in arc tube.

Figure 14-7. Test light for a 120V household circuits contains a neon light.

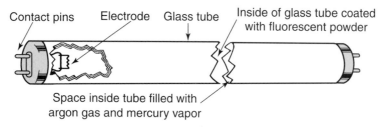

Contact pins   Electrode   Glass tube   Inside of glass tube coated
with fluorescent powder

Space inside tube filled with
argon gas and mercury vapor

Figure 14-8. Construction of a typical fluorescent lamp.

Unlike incandescent lamps, fluorescent lamps cannot control their current consumption. Unless the current is controlled, the lamp burns itself out immediately. To avoid this, ballasts (devices that limit current to the proper operating value) are wired into the fluorescent circuit.

Small fluorescent lamps require choke ballasts to limit current input to prevent burnout. Large lamps require both a choke coil and a transformer. The transformer steps up the voltage and the coil limits the current.

Compact fluorescent bulbs, **Figure 14-9,** can be screwed into standard incandescent bulb outlets. They have become popular for their long life and energy efficiency. Although they are considerably more expensive than incandescent bulbs, when placed in lamps that are used heavily, they recoup their costs quickly.

Figure 14-9. Fluorescent lamp.

Simple Specification Form

The following material is intended as a guide to preparing wiring specifications for dwellings.

All outlets, the locations of wall switches, and the outlet or outlets controlled by each switch should be shown clearly on the floor plans that must be considered as an essential part of the plans, or contract.

SPECIFICATIONS FOR ELECTRIC WIRING IN THE DWELLING TO BE ERECTED AT _____ FOR _____

1. GENERAL

The installation of electric wiring and equipment shall conform with local regulations, the National Electrical Code, and the requirements of the local electric service company. All materials shall be new and shall be listed by Underwriters' Laboratories, Incorporated, as conforming to its standards, in every case where such a standard has been established for the particular type of material in question.

2. GUARANTEE

The contractor shall leave his work in proper order and, without additional charge, replace any work or material that develops defects, except from ordinary wear and tear, within one year from the date of the final certificate of approval.

3. WIRING METHODS

Interior wiring shall be _____. No exposed wiring shall be installed except in unfinished portions of basement, utility room, garage, attic, and other spaces that may be unfinished.

4. SERVICE ENTRANCE conductors shall be three No. _____ wires.

(Fill in wiring method)

5. SERVICE-EQUIPMENT shall consist of_____

---

6. TWENTY-AMPERE BRANCH CIRCUITS

At least _____ 20-ampere branch circuits shall be installed to supply all lighting outlets and all convenience outlets except those that are supplied by appliance branch circuits. The total number of outlets shall as nearly as possible be divided equally between these circuits. In each living room, library, sunroom, bedroom, and each other principal room, the outlets shall be divided between two or more branch circuits. One 20-ampere branch circuit shall be installed to supply all outlets for laundry requirements.

7. BEDROOM CIRCUITS

All bedroom outlets shall be protected by an arc-fault circuit interrupter.

8. APPLIANCE BRANCH CIRCUITS

Two appliance branch circuits shall be installed to supply all convenience outlets in the dining room, breakfast room, kitchen, and pantry. These circuits shall be so installed that convenience outlets served by both circuits will be available in both the kitchen and the laundry.

9. BRANCH CIRCUIT EQUIPMENT shall be _____

_____

(Fill in type of equipment)

10. OUTLETS AND SWITCHES

Lighting outlets, convenience outlets complete with receptacles, and switches shall be installed as shown on the plans.

Unless otherwise shown on plans, the height of outlets above floor shall be approximately:

Switches .... 48 inches
Convenience outlets .... 18 inches

11. SPECIAL PURPOSE OUTLETS AND CIRCUITS shall be installed as shown on the plans. The circuits shall be:

Circuits for	No. of wires	Size
_____	_____	_____
_____	_____	_____
_____	_____	_____
_____	_____	_____

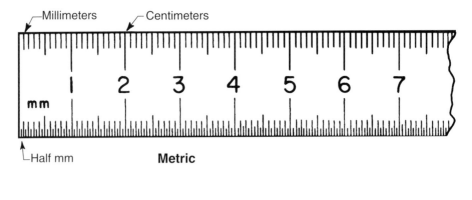

Metric

Fractional Inch

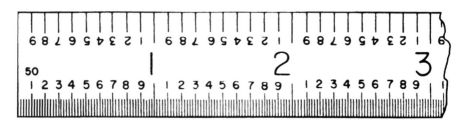

Decimal Inch

This drawing compares a metric (millimeter) rule with the conventional fractional and decimal inch rules. For conversion; 1 yard = 0.914 meters, 1 foot = 30.480 centimeters, and 1 inch 2.540 centimeters. Also, for conversion; 1 meter = 3.281 feet, and 1 centimeter 0.3937 inch.

Useful Tables from the National Electrical Code

The following tables are taken from the 2005 edition of the National Electrical Code. These tables contain information you may find useful when installing residential wiring. Please note that this material is not the complete and official position of the National Fire Protection Association on the referenced subject, which is represented only by the standard in its entirety.

Table 210.24 Summary of Branch-Circuit Requirements

Circuit Rating	15 A	20 A	30 A	40 A	50 A
Conductors (min. size):					
Circuit wires[1]	14	12	10	8	6
Taps	14	14	14	12	12
Fixture wires and cords— See Section 240.5					
Overcurrent Protection	**15 A**	**20 A**	**30 A**	**40 A**	**50 A**
Outlet Devices:					
Lampholders permitted	Any type	Any type	Heavy duty	Heavy duty	Heavy duty
Receptacle rating[2]	15 max. A	15 or 20 A	30 A	40 or 50 A	50 A
Maximum Load	**15 A**	**20 A**	**30 A**	**40 A**	**50 A**
Permissible load	See Section 210.23(A)	See Section 210.23(A)	See Section 210.23(B)	See Section 210.23(C)	See Section 210.23(C)

[1]These gauges are for copper conductors.
[2]For receptacle rating of cord-connected electric-discharge luminaires (lighting fixtures), see Section 410.30(C).

General Lighting Loads by Occupancies

Type of Occupancy	Unit Load per Square Foot (Volt-Amperes)
Armories and auditoriums	1
Banks	3½
Barber shops and beauty parlors	3
Churches	1
Clubs	2
Court rooms	2
Dwelling units	3
Garages—commercial (storage)	½
Hospitals	2
Hotels and motels, including apartment houses without provision for cooking by tenants\`	2
Industrial commercial (loft) buildings	2
Lodge rooms	1½
Office buildings	3½
Restaurants	2
Schools	3
Stores	3
Warehouses (storage)	¼
In any of the above occupancies except one-family dwellings and individual dwelling units of two-family and multifamily dwellings:	
Assembly halls and auditoriums	1
Halls, corridors, closets, stairways	½
Storage spaces	¼

In addition, a unit load of 1 volt-ampere per square foot shall be included for general-purpose receptacle outlets where the actual number of general-purpose receptacle outlets is unknown.

Based on Table 220.12 from the NEC.

Table 220.42 Lighting Load Demand Factors

Type of Occupancy	Portion of Lighting Load to Which Demand Factor Applies (Volt-Amperes)	Demand Factor (Percent)
Dwelling units	First 3000 or less at	100
	From 3001 to 120,000 at	35
	Remainder over 120,000 at	25
Hospitals*	First 50,000 or less at	40
	Remainder over 50,000 at	20
Hotels and motels, including apartment houses without provision for cooking by tenants*	First 20,000 or less at	50
	From 20,001 to 100,000 at	40
	Remainder over 100,000 at	30
Warehouses (storage)	First 12,500 or less at	100
	Remainder over 12,500 at	50
All others	Total volt-amperes	100

*The demand factors of this table shall not apply to the computed load of feeders or services supplying areas in hospitals, hotels, and motels where the entire lighting is likely to be used at one time, as in operating rooms, ballrooms, or dining rooms.

Table 220.54 Demand Factors for Household Electric Clothes Dryers

Number of Dryers	Demand Factor (Percent)
1-4	100%
5	85%
6	75%
7	65%
8	60%
9	55%
10	50%
11	47%
12-22	% = 47 − (number of dryers − 11)
23	35%
24-42	% = 35 − [0.5 × (number of dryers − 23)]
43 and over	25%

Table 220.55 Demand Factors and Loads for Household Electric Ranges, Wall-Mounted Ovens, Counter-Mounted Cooking Units, and Other Household Cooking Appliances over 1¾ kW Rating (Column C to be used in all cases except as otherwise permitted in Note 3.)

Number of Appliances	Demand Factor (Percent) (See Notes)		
	Column A (Less than 3½ kW Rating)	Column B (3½ kW to 8¾ kW Rating)	Column C (Maximun Demand (kW) (See Notes) (Not over 12 kw Rating)
1	80	80	8
2	75	65	11
3	70	55	14
4	66	50	17
5	62	45	20
6	59	43	21
7	56	40	22
8	53	36	23
9	51	35	24
10	49	34	25
11	47	32	26
12	45	32	27
13	43	32	28
14	41	32	29
15	40	32	30
16	39	28	31
17	38	28	32
18	37	28	33
19	36	28	34
20	35	28	35
21	34	26	36
22	33	26	37
23	32	26	38
24	31	26	39
25	30	26	40
26–30	30	24	15 kW + 1 kW for each range
31–40	30	22	
41–50	30	20	25 kW + ¾ kW for each range
51–60	30	18	
61 and over	30	16	

Based on NEC Table 220.55.

Table 250.66 Grounding Electrode Conductor for Alternating-Current Systems

Size of Largest Service-Entrance Conductor or Equivalent Area for Parallel Conductors		Size of Grounding Electrode Conductor	
Copper	Aluminum or Copper-Clad Aluminum	Copper	Aluminum or Copper-Clad Aluminum[b]
2 or smaller	1/Ø or smaller	8	6
1 or 1/0	2/0 or 3/0	6	4
2/0 or 3/0	4/0 or 250 kcmil	4	2
Over 3/0 through 350 kcmil	Over 250 kcmil through 500 kcmil	2	1/0
Over 350 kcmil through 600 kcmil	Over 500 kcmil through 900 kcmil	1/0	3/0
Over 600 kcmil through 1100 kcmil	Over 900 kcmil through 1750 kcmil	2/0	4/0
Over 1100 kcmil	Over 1750 kcmil	3/0	250 kcmil

1. Where multiple sets of service-entrance conductors are used as permitted in Section 230.40, Exception No. 2, the equivalent size of the largest sum of the areas of the corresponding conductors of each set.

2. Where there are no service-entrance conductors, the grounding electrode conductor size shall be determined by the equivalent size of the largest service-entrance conductor required for the load to be served.

[a]This table also applies to the derived conductors of separately derived ac systems.

[b]See installation restrictions in Section 250.64(A).

Table 250.122 Minimum Size Equipment Grounding Conductors for Grounding Raceway and Equipment

Rating or Setting of Automatic Overcurrent Device in Circuit Ahead of Equipment, Conduit, etc., Not Exceeding (Amperes)	Size (AWG or kcmil)	
	Copper	Aluminum or Copper-Clad Aluminum*
15	14	12
20	12	10
30	10	8
40	10	8
60	10	8
100	8	6
200	6	4
300	4	2
400	3	1
500	2	1/0
600	1	2/0
800	1/0	3/0
1000	2/0	4/0
1200	3/0	250
1600	4/0	350
2000	250	400
2500	350	600
3000	400	600
4000	500	800
5000	700	1200
6000	800	1200

Note: Where necessary to comply with Sections 250.4(A)(5) or 250.4(B)(4), the equipment grounding conductor shall be sized larger than specified in this table.
*See installation restrictions in Section 250.120.

Minimum Cover Requirements, based on NEC Table 300.5 (in Inches)

Location of Wiring Method or Circuit	Type of Wiring Method or Circuit				
	Column 1 Direct Burial Cables or Conductors	Column 2 Rigid Metal Conduit or Intermediate Metal Conduit	Column 3 Nonmetallic Raceways Listed for Direct Burial Without Concrete Encasement or Other Approved Raceways	Column 4 Residential Branch Circuits Rated 120 Volts or Less with GFCI Protection and Maximum Overcurrent Protection of 20 Amperes	Column 5 Circuits for Control of Irrigation and Landscape Lighting Limited to Not More than 30 Volts and Installed with Type UF or in Other Identified Cable or Raceway
All locations not specified below	24	6	18	12	6
In trench below 2-in. thick concrete or equivalent	18	6	12	6	6
Under a building	0 (in raceway only)	0	0	0 (in raceway only)	0 (in raceway only)
Under minimum of 4-in. thick concrete exterior slab with no vehicular traffic and the slab extending not less than 6 in. beyond the underground installation	18	4	4	6 (direct burial) 4 (in raceway)	6
Under streets, highways, roads, alleys, driveways, and parking lots	24	24	24	24	24

Minimum Cover Requirements *(continued)*

	Type of Wiring Method or Circuit				
Location of Wiring Method or Circuit	Column 1 Direct Burial Cables or Conductors	Column 2 Rigid Metal Conduit or Intermediate Metal Conduit	Column 3 Nonmetallic Raceways Listed for Direct Burial Without Concrete Encasement or Other Approved Raceways	Column 4 Residential Branch Circuits Rated 120 Volts or Less with GFCI Protection and Maximum Overcurrent Protection of 20 Amperes	Column 5 Circuits for Control of Irrigation and Landscape Lighting Limited to Not More than 30 Volts and Installed with Type UF or in Other Identified Cable or Raceway
One- and two-family dwelling driveways and outdoor parking areas, and used only for dwelling-related purposes	18	18	18	12	18
In or under airport runways, including adjacent areas where trespassing prohibited	18	18	18	18	18

Refer to the NEC for complete information.

Conductor Application and Insulations

Trade Name	Type Letter	Maximum Operating Temperature	Application Provisions	Insulation	Thickness of Insulation		Outer Covering[1]
					AWG or kcmil	Mils	
Fluorinated ethylene propylene	FEP or FEPB	90°C 194°F	Dry and damp locations	Fluorinated ethylene propylene	14-10 8-2	20 30	None
		200°C 392°F	Dry locations — special applications[2]	Fluorinated ethylene propylene	14-8	14	Glass braid
					6-2	14	Glass or other suitable braid material
Mineral insulation (metal sheathed)	MI	90°C 194°F 250°C 482°F	Dry and wet locations For special applications[2]	Magnesium oxide	18-16[3] 16-10 9-4 3-500	23 36 50 55	Copper or alloy steel

[1]Some insulations do not require an outer covering.
[2]Where design conditions require maximum conductor operating temperatures above 90°C (194°F).
[3]For signaling circuits permitting 300-volt insulation.

Based on NEC Table 310.13. Refer to the NEC for complete information.

Conductor Application and Insulations *(continued)*

Trade Name	Type Letter	Maximum Operating Temperature	Application Provisions	Insulation	Thickness of Insulation AWG or kcmil	Mils	Outer Covering[1]
Moisture-, heat-, and oil-resistant thermoplastic	MTW	60°C 140°F 90°C 194°F	Machine tool wiring in wet locations as permitted in NFPA 79 (see Article 670) Machine tool wiring in dry locations as permitted in NFPA 79 (see Article 670)	Flame-retardant moisture-, heat-, and oil-resistant thermoplastic	22-12 10 8 6 4-2 1-4/0 213-500 591-1000	(A) (B) 30 15 30 20 45 30 60 30 60 40 80 50 95 60 110 70	(A) None (B) Nylon jacket or equivalent
Paper		85°C 185°F	For underground service conductors, or by special permission	Paper			Lead sheath
Perfluoroalkoxy	PFA	90°C 194°F 200°C 392°F	Dry and damp locations Dry locations — special applications[2]	Perfluoroalkoxy	14-10 8-2 1-4/0	20 30 45	None

[1] Some insulations do not require an outer covering.

[2] Where design conditions require maximum conductor operating temperatures above 90°C (194°F).

Conductor Application and Insulations *(continued)*

Trade Name	Type Letter	Maximum Operating Temperature	Application Provisions	Insulation	Thickness of Insulation AWG or kcmil	Mils	Outer Covering[1]
Perfluoroalkoxy	PFAH	250°C 482°F	Dry locations only. Only for leads within apparatus or within raceways connected to apparatus. (Nickel or nickel-coated copper only)	Perfluoroalkoxy	14-10 8-2 1-4/0	20 30 45	None
Thermoset	RHH	90°C 194°F	Dry and damp locations		14-10 8-2 1-4/0 213-500 501-1000 1001-2000 For 601-2000, see Table 310-62	45 60 80 95 110 125	Moisture-resistant, flame-retardant, non-metallic covering[1]

[1]Some insulations do not require an outer covering.

Conductor Application and Insulations *(continued)*

Trade Name	Type Letter	Maximum Operating Temperature	Application Provisions	Insulation	Thickness of Insulation		Outer Covering[1]
					AWG or kcmil	Mils	
Moisture-resistant thermoset	RHW[2]	75°C 167°F	Dry and wet locations Where over 2000 volts insulation, shall be ozone-resistant	Flame-retardant, moisture-resistant thermoset	14-10 8-2 1-4/0 213-500 501-1000 1001-2000 For 601-2000 volts, see Table 310-62	45 60 80 95 110 125	Moisture-resistant, flame-retardant, non-metallic covering[3]
Moisture-resistant thermoset	RHW-2	90°C 194°F	Dry and wet locations	Flame-retardant, moisture-resistant thermoset	14-10 8-2 1-4/0 213-500 501-1000 1001-2000 For 601-2000 volts, see Table 310-62	45 60 80 95 110 125	Moisture-resistant, flame-retardant, non-metallic covering[3]

[1]Some insulations do not require an outer covering.

[2]Listed wire types designated with the suffix "–2," such as RHW-2, shall be permitted to be used at a continuous 90°C (194°F)-operating temperature, wet or dry.

[3]Some rubber insulations do not require an outer covering.

Conductor Application and Insulations *(continued)*

Trade Name	Type Letter	Maximum Operating Temperature	Application Provisions	Insulation	Thickness of Insulation		Outer Covering[1]
					AWG or kcmil	Mils	
Silicone	SA	90°C 194°F	Dry and damp locations	Silicone rubber	14-10	45	Glass or other suitable braid material
					8-2	60	
		200°C 392°F	For special application[2]		1-4/0	80	
					213-500	95	
					501-1000	110	
					1001-2000	125	
Thermoset	SIS	90°C 194°F	Switchboard wiring only	Flame-retardant thermoset	14-10	30	None
					8-2	45	
					1-4/0	95	
Thermoplastic and fibrous outer braid	TBS	90°C 194°F	Switchboard wiring only	Thermoplastic	14-10	30	Flame-retardant, nonmetallic covering
					8	45	
					6-2	60	
					1-4/0	80	

[1]Some insulations do not require an outer covering.
[2]Where design conditions require maximum conductor operating temperatures above 90°C (194°F).

Conductor Application and Insulations *(continued)*

Trade Name	Type Letter	Maximum Operating Temperature	Application Provisions	Insulation	Thickness of Insulation		Outer Covering¹
					AWG or kcmil	Mils	
Extended poly-trafluoro-ethylene	TFE	250°C 482°F	Dry locations only. Only for leads within apparatus or within raceways connected to apparatus, or as open wiring (Nickel or nickel-coated copper only)	Extruded poly-tetrafluoro-ethylene	14-10 8-2 1-4/0	20 30 45	None
Heat-resistant thermoplastic	THHN	90°C 194°F	Dry and damp locations	Flame-retardant, heat-resistant thermoplastic	14-12 10 8-6 4-2 1-4/0 250-500 501-1000	15 20 30 40 50 60 70	Nylon jacket or equivalent
Moisture- and heat-resistant thermoplastic	THHW	75°C 167°F 90°C 194°F	Wet location Dry location	Flame-retardant, moisture- and heat-resistant thermoplastic	14-10 8 6-2 1-4/0 213-500 501-1000	30 45 60 80 95 110	None

¹Some insulations do not require an outer covering.

Conductor Application and Insulations *(continued)*

Trade Name	Type Letter	Maximum Operating Temperature	Application Provisions	Insulation	Thickness of Insulation		Outer Covering[1]
					AWG or kcmil	Mils	
Moisture- and heat-resistant thermoplastic	THW[a]	75°C 167°F 90°C 194°F	Dry and wet locations. Special applications within electric discharge lighting equipment. Limited to 1000 open-circuit volts or less (Size 14-8 only as permitted in Section 410-31)	Flame-retardant, moisture- and heat-resistant thermoplastic	14-10 8 6-2 1-4/0 213-500 501-1000 1001-2000	30 45 60 80 95 110 125	None
Moisture- and heat-resistant thermoplastic	THWN[a]	75°C 167°F	Dry and wet locations	Flame-retardant, moisture- and heat-resistant thermoplastic	14-12 10 8-6 4-2 1-4/0 250-500 501-1000	15 20 30 40 50 60 70	Nylon jacket or equivalent

[1]Some insulations do not require an outer covering.
[a]Listed wire types designated with the suffix "-2," such as RHW-2, shall be permitted to be used at a continuous 90°C (194°F)-operating temperature, wet or dry.

Conductor Application and Insulations (continued)

Trade Name	Type Letter	Maximum Operating Temperature	Application Provisions	Insulation	Thickness of Insulation		Outer Covering[1]
					AWG or kcmil	Mils	
Moisture-resistant thermoplastic	TW	60°C 140°F	Dry and wet locations	Flame-retardant, moisture-resistant thermoplastic	14-10 8 6-2 1-4/0 213-500 501-1000 1001-2000	30 45 60 80 95 110 125	None
Underground feeder and branch-circuit cable—single conductor (For Type UF cable employing more than one conductor, see Article 339)	UF	60°C 140°F	See Article 340	Moisture-resistant	14-10 8-2 1-4/0	60[2] 80[2] 95[2]	Integral with insulation
		75°C 167°F		Moisture- and heat-resistant			

[1]Some insulations do not require an outer covering.
[2]Includes integral jacket.
[3]For ampacity limitation, see Section 340.80.

Conductor Application and Insulations (continued)

Trade Name	Type Letter	Maximum Operating Temperature	Application Provisions	Insulation	Thickness of Insulation		Outer Covering[¹]
					AWG or kcmil	Mils	
Underground service-entrance cable—single conductor (For Type USE cable employing more than one conductor, see Article 338)	USE[¹]	75°C 167°F	See Article 338	Heat- and moisture resistant	14-10 8-2 1-4/0 213-500 501-1000 1001-2000	45 60 80 95[²] 110 125	Moisture-resistant nonmetallic covering [see Section 338.2]

[¹]Some insulations do not require an outer covering.
[¹]Listed wire types designated with the suffix "-2," such as RHW-2, shall be permitted to be used at a continuous 90°C (194°F)-operating temperature, wet or dry.
[²]Insulation thickness shall be permitted to be 80 mils for listed Type USE conductors that have been subjected to special investigations. The nonmetallic covering over individual rubber-covered conductors of aluminum-sheathed cable and of lead-sheathed or multiconductor cable shall not be required to be flame retardant. For Type MC cable, see Section 334-20. For nonmetallic-sheathed cable, see Section 336-30. For Type UF cable, see Section 339-1.

Conductor Application and Insulations (continued)

Trade Name	Type Letter	Maximum Operating Temperature	Application Provisions	Insulation	Thickness of Insulation		Outer Covering¹
					AWG or kcmil	Mils	
Thermoset	XHH	90°C 194°F	Dry and damp locations	Flame-retardant thermoset	14-10	30	None
					8-2	45	
					1-4/0	55	
					213-500	65	
					501-1000	80	
					1001-2000	95	
Moisture-resistant thermoset	XHHW¹	90°C 194°F 75°C 167°F	Dry and damp locations Wet locations	Flame-retardant, moisture-resistant thermoset	14-10	30	None
					8-2	45	
					1-4/0	55	
					213-500	65	
					501-1000	80	
					1001-2000	95	
Moisture-resistant thermoset	XHHW-2	90°C 194°F	Dry and wet locations	Flame-retardant, moisture-resistant thermoset	14-10	30	None
					8-2	45	
					1-4/0	55	
					213-500	65	
					501-1000	80	
					1001-2000	95	

¹Some insulations do not require an outer covering.
¹Listed wire types designated with the suffix "-2," such as RHW-2, shall be permitted to be used at a continuous 90°C (194°F)-operating temperature, wet or dry.

Conductor Application and Insulations (*continued*)

Trade Name	Type Letter	Maximum Operating Temperature	Application Provisions	Insulation	Thickness of Insulation AWG or kcmil	Mils	Outer Covering[1]
Modified ethylene tetrafluoro-ethylene	Z	90°C 194°F 150°C 302°F	Dry and damp locations Dry locations—special applications[2]	Modified ethylene tetrafluoro-ethylene	14-12 10 8-4 3-1 1/0-4/0	15 20 25 35 45	None
Modified ethylene tetrafluoro-ethylene	ZW[3]	75°C 167°F 90°C 194°F 150°C 302°F	Wet locations Dry and damp locations Dry locations—special applications	Modified ethylene tetrafluoro-ethylene	14-10 8-2	30 45	None

[1] Some insulations do not require an outer covering.
[2] Where design conditions require maximum conductor operating temperatures above 90°C (194°F).
[3] Listed wire types designated with the suffix "-2," such as RHW-2, shall be permitted to be used at a continuous 90°C (194°F)-operating temperature, wet or dry.

Table 310.15(B)(6). Conductor Types and Sizes for 120/240-Volt, 3-Wire, Single-Phase Dwelling Services and Feeders. Conductor Types RHH, RHW, RHW-2, THHN, THHW, THW, THW-2, THWN, THWN-2, XHHW, XHHW-2, SE, USE, USE-2.

Conductor (AWG or kcmil)		Service or Feeder Rating (Amperes)
Copper	Aluminum or Copper-Clad Aluminum	
4	2	100
3	1	110
2	1/0	125
1	2/0	150
1/0	3/0	175
2/0	4/0	200
3/0	250	225
4/0	300	250
250	350	300
350	500	350
400	600	400

Table 310.16 Allowable Ampacities of Insulated Conductors Rated 0 Through 2000 Volts, 60°C Through 90°C (140°F Through 194°F), Not More than Three Current-Carrying Conductors in Raceway, Cable, or Earth (Directly Buried), Based on Ambient Temperature of 30°C (86°F)

Size AWG or kcmil	Temperature Rating of Conductor (See Table 310.13.)						Size AWG or kcmil
	60°C (140°F)	75°C (167°F)	90°C (194°F)	60°C (140°F)	75°C (167°F)	90°C (194°F)	
	Types TW, UF	Types RHW, THHW, THW, THWN, XHHW, USE, ZW	Types TBS, SA, SIS, FEP, FEPB, MI, RHH, RHW-2, THHN, THHW, THW-2, THWN-2, USE-2, XHH, XHHW, XHHW-2, ZW-2	Types TW, UF	Types RHW, THHW, THW, THWN, USE	Types TBS, SA, SIS, THHN, THHW, THW-2, THWN-2, RHH, RHW-2, USE-2, XHH, XHHW, XHHW-2, ZW-2	
	COPPER			ALUMINUM OR COPPER-CLAD ALUMINUM			
18	—	—	14	—	—	—	—
16	—	—	18	—	—	—	—
14*	20	20	25	—	—	—	—
12*	25	25	30	20	20	25	12*
10*	30	35	40	25	30	35	10*
8	40	50	55	30	40	45	8
6	55	65	75	40	50	60	6
4	70	85	95	55	65	75	4
3	85	100	110	65	75	85	3
2	95	115	130	75	90	100	2
1	110	130	150	85	100	115	1
1/0	125	150	170	100	120	135	1/0
2/0	145	175	195	115	135	150	2/0
3/0	165	200	225	130	155	175	3/0
4/0	195	230	260	150	180	205	4/0
250	215	255	290	170	205	230	250
300	240	285	320	190	230	255	300
350	260	310	350	210	250	280	350
400	280	335	380	225	270	305	400
500	320	380	430	260	310	350	500
600	355	420	475	285	340	385	600
700	385	460	520	310	375	420	700
750	400	475	535	320	385	435	750
800	410	490	555	330	395	450	800
900	435	520	585	355	425	480	900
1000	455	545	615	375	445	500	1000
1250	495	590	665	405	485	545	1250
1500	520	625	705	435	520	585	1500
1750	545	650	735	455	545	615	1750
2000	560	665	750	470	560	630	2000

CORRECTION FACTORS

Ambient Temp. (°C)	For ambient temperatures other than 30°C (86°F), multiply the allowable ampacities shown above by the appropriate factor shown below.						Ambient Temp. (°F)
21–25	1.08	1.05	1.04	1.08	1.05	1.04	70–77
26–30	1.00	1.00	1.00	1.00	1.00	1.00	78–86
31–35	0.91	0.94	0.96	0.91	0.94	0.96	87–95
36–40	0.82	0.88	0.91	0.82	0.88	0.91	96–104
41–45	0.71	0.82	0.87	0.71	0.82	0.87	105–113
46–50	0.58	0.75	0.82	0.58	0.75	0.82	114–122
51–55	0.41	0.67	0.76	0.41	0.67	0.76	123–131
56–60	—	0.58	0.71	—	0.58	0.71	132–140
61–70	—	0.33	0.58	—	0.33	0.58	141–158
71–80	—	—	0.41	—	—	0.41	159–176

* See 240.4(D).

Table 310.16 contains allowable conductor ampacity for an ambient temperature of 86°F when three or less conductors are contained in a raceway. Correction factors are used to adjust the values when there is a different ambient temperature or if there are more than three conductors in the raceway.

Table 310.18 Allowable Ampacities of Three Single-Insulated Conductors Rated 0 Through 2000 Volts, 150°C Through 250°C (302°F Through 482°F), in Raceway or Cable, Based on Ambient Air Temperature of 40°C (104°F)

Size	Temperature Rating of Conductor (see Table 310-13)				Size
	150°C (302°F)	200°C (392°F)	250°C (482°F)	150°C (302°F)	
AWG or kcmil	Type Z	Types FEP, FEPB, PFA	Types PFAH, TFE,	Type Z	AWG or kcmi
		COPPER	NICKEL OR NICKEL-COATED COPPER	ALUMINUM OR COPPER-CLAD ALUMINUM	
14	34	36	39	—	14
12	43	45	54	30	12
10	55	60	73	44	10
8	76	83	93	57	8
6	96	110	117	75	6
4	120	125	148	94	4
3	143	152	166	109	3
2	160	171	191	124	2
1	186	197	215	145	1
1/0	215	229	244	169	1/0
2/0	251	260	273	198	2/0
3/0	288	297	308	227	3/0
4/0	332	346	361	260	4/0

CORRECTION FACTORS

Ambient Temp. (°C)	For ambient temperatures other than 40°C (104°F), multiply the allowable ampacities shown above by the appropriate factor shown below.				Ambient Temp. (°F)
41–50	0.95	0.97	0.98	0.95	105–122
51–60	0.90	0.94	0.95	0.90	123–140
61–70	0.85	0.90	0.93	0.85	141–158
71–80	0.80	0.87	0.90	0.80	159–176
81–90	0.74	0.83	0.87	0.74	177–194
91–100	0.67	0.79	0.85	0.67	195–212
101–120	0.52	0.71	0.79	0.52	213–248
121–140	0.30	0.61	0.72	0.30	249–284
141–160	—	0.50	0.65	—	285–320
161–180	—	0.35	0.58	—	321–356
181–200	—	—	0.49	—	357–392
201–225	—	—	0.35	—	393–437

Table 310.18 contains allowable conductor ampacity for an ambient temperature of 104°F when three or less conductors are contained in a raceway. Correction factors are used to adjust the values when there is a different ambient temperature or if there are more than three conductors in the raceway.

Spacings for Conductor Supports

Size of Wire	Support of Conductors in Vertical Raceways	Conductors	
		Aluminum or Copper-Clad Aluminum	Copper
18 AWG through 8 AWG	Not greater than	100 ft.	100 ft.
6 AWG through 1/0 AWG	Not greater than	200 ft.	100 ft.
2/0 AWG through 4/0 AWG	Not greater than	180 ft.	80 ft.
Over 4/0 AWG through 350 kcmil	Not greater than	135 ft.	60 ft.
Over 350 kcmil through 500 kcmil	Not greater than	120 ft.	50 ft.
Over 500 kcmil through 750 kcmil	Not greater than	95 ft.	40 ft.
Over 750 kcmil	Not greater than	85 ft.	35 ft.

Note: For SI units, 1 ft = 0.3048 m.

Based on NEC Table 300.19(A). Refer to the NEC for complete information.

Radius of Conduit and Tubing Bends

One Shot and Full Shoe		
Conduit or Tubing Size (in.)	**Benders (in.)**	**Other Bends (in.)**
½	4	4
¾	4½	5
1	5¾	6
1¼	7¼	8
1½	8¼	10
2	9½	12
2½	10½	15
3	13	18
3½	15	21
4	16	24
5	24	30
6	30	36

Based on NEC Chapter 9, Table 2. Refer to the NEC for complete information.

Supports for Rigid Metal Conduit

Conduit Size (in.)	Maximum Distance Between Rigid Metal Conduit Supports (ft)
½–¾	10
1	12
1¼–1½	14
2–2½	16
3 and larger	20

Note: For SI units, 1 ft = 0.3048 m (supports).
Based on NEC Table 344.30(B)(2). Refer to the NEC for complete information.

Table 344.22. Maximum Number of Insulated Conductors in ³⁄₈-in. Flexible Metal Conduit*

Size (AWG)	Types RFH-2, SF-2		Types TF, XHHW, TW		Types TFN, THHN, THWN		Types FEP, FEPB, PF, PGF	
	Fittings Inside Conduit	Fittings Outside Conduit	Fittings Inside Conduit	Fittings Outside Conduit	Fittings Inside Conduit	Fittings Outside Conduit	Fittings Inside Conduit	Fittings Outside Conduit
18	2	3	3	5	5	8	5	8
16	1	2	3	4	4	6	4	6
14	1	2	2	3	3	4	3	4
12	—	—	1	2	2	3	2	3
10	—	—	1	1	1	1	1	2

*In addition, one covered or bare equipment grounding conductor of the same size shall be permitted.

Table 314.16(A) Metal Boxes

Box Trade Size			Minimum Volume		Maximum Number of Conductors*						
mm	**in.**		**cm.³**	**in.³**	**18**	**16**	**14**	**12**	**10**	**8**	**6**
100 × 32	(4 × 1¼)	round/octagonal	205	12.5	8	7	6	5	5	5	2
100 × 38	(4 × 1½)	round/octagonal	254	15.5	10	8	7	6	6	5	3
100 × 54	(4 × 2⅛)	round/octagonal	353	21.5	14	12	10	9	8	7	4
100 × 32	(4 × 1¼)	square	295	18.0	12	10	9	8	7	6	3
100 × 38	(4 × 1½)	square	344	21.0	14	12	10	9	8	7	4
100 × 54	(4 × 2⅛)	square	497	30.3	20	17	15	13	12	10	6
120 × 32	(4¹¹⁄₁₆ × 1¼)	square	418	25.5	17	14	12	11	10	8	5
120 × 38	(4¹¹⁄₁₆ × 1½)	square	484	29.5	19	16	14	13	11	9	5
120 × 54	(4¹¹⁄₁₆ × 2⅛)	square	689	42.0	28	24	21	18	16	14	8
75 × 50 × 38	(3 × 2 × 1½)	device	123	7.5	5	4	3	3	3	2	1
75 × 50 × 50	(3 × 2 × 2)	device	164	10.0	6	5	5	4	4	3	2
75 × 50 × 57	(3 × 2 × 2¼)	device	172	10.5	7	6	5	4	4	3	2
75 × 50 × 65	(3 × 2 × 2½)	device	205	12.5	8	7	6	5	5	4	2
75 × 50 × 70	(3 × 2 × 2¾)	device	230	14.0	9	8	7	6	5	4	2
75 × 50 × 90	(3 × 2 × 3½)	device	295	18.0	12	10	9	8	7	6	3
100 × 54 × 38	(4 × 2⅛ × 1½)	device	169	10.3	6	5	5	4	4	3	2
100 × 54 × 48	(4 × 2⅛ × 1⅞)	device	213	13.0	8	7	6	5	5	4	2
100 × 54 × 54	(4 × 2⅛ × 2⅛)	device	238	14.5	9	8	7	6	5	4	2
95 × 50 × 65	(3¾ × 2 × 2½)	masonry box/gang	230	14.0	9	8	7	6	5	4	2
95 × 50 × 90	(3¾ × 2 × 3½)	masonry box/gang	344	21.0	14	12	10	9	8	7	2
min. 44.5 depth	FS — single cover/gang (1¾)		221	13.5	9	7	6	6	5	4	2
min. 60.3 depth	FD — single cover/gang (2⅜)		295	18.0	12	10	9	8	7	6	3
min. 44.5 depth	FS — multiple cover/gang (1¾)		295	18.0	12	10	9	8	7	6	3
min. 60.3 depth	FD — multiple cover/gang (2⅜)		395	24.0	16	13	12	10	9	8	4

*Where no volume allowances are required by 314.16(B)(2) through 314.16(B)(5).

Volume Allowance Required per Conductor

Size of Conductor (AWG)	Free Space Within Box for Each Conductor (in.')
18	1.50
16	1.75
14	2.00
12	2.25
10	2.50
8	3.00
6	5.00

Based on NEC Table 314.16(B). Refer to the NEC for complete information.

Dimensions and Percent Area of Conduit and Tubing

Electrical Metallic Tubing

Trade Size (in.)	Internal Diameter (in.)	Total Area 100% (in.²)	2 Wires 31% (in.²)	Over 2 Wires 40% (in.²)	1 Wire 53% (in.²)
½	0.622	0.304	0.094	0.122	0.161
¾	0.824	0.533	0.165	0.213	0.283
1	1.049	0.864	0.268	0.346	0.458
1¼	1.380	1.496	0.464	0.598	0.793
1½	1.610	2.036	0.631	0.814	1.079
2	2.067	3.356	1.040	1.342	1.778
2½	2.731	5.858	1.816	2.343	3.105
3	3.356	8.846	2.742	3.538	4.688
3½	3.834	11.545	3.579	4.618	6.119
4	4.334	14.753	4.573	5.901	7.819

Electrical Nonmetallic Tubing

Trade Size (in.)	Internal Diameter (in.)	Total Area 100% (in.²)	2 Wires 31% (in.²)	Over 2 Wires 40% (in.²)	1 Wire 53% (in.²)
½	0.560	0.246	0.076	0.099	0.131
¾	0.760	0.454	0.141	0.181	0.240
1	1.000	0.785	0.243	0.314	0.416
1¼	1.340	1.410	0.437	0.564	0.747
1½	1.570	1.936	0.600	0.774	1.026
2	2.020	3.205	0.994	1.282	1.699
2½	—	—	—	—	—
3	—	—	—	—	—
3½	—	—	—	—	—
4	—	—	—	—	—

Flexible Metal Conduit

Trade Size (in.)	Internal Diameter (in.)	Total Area 100% (in.²)	2 Wires 31% (in.²)	Over 2 Wires 40% (in.²)	1 Wire 53% (in.²)
⅜	0.384	0.116	0.036	0.046	0.061
½	0.635	0.317	0.098	0.127	0.168
¾	0.824	0.533	0.165	0.213	0.282
1	1.020	0.817	0.253	0.327	0.433
1¼	1.275	1.277	0.396	0.511	0.677
1½	1.538	1.857	0.576	0.743	0.984
2	2.040	3.269	1.013	1.307	1.732
2½	2.500	4.909	1.522	1.964	2.602
3	3.000	7.069	2.191	2.827	3.746
3½	3.500	9.621	2.983	3.848	5.099
4	4.000	12.566	3.896	5.027	6.660

Based on NEC Table 4, Chapter 9. Refer to the NEC for complete information.

Dimensions and Percent Area of Conduit and Tubing *(continued)*

Intermediate Metal Conduit

Trade Size (in.)	Internal Diameter (in.)	Total Area 100% (in.²)	2 Wires 31% (in.²)	Over 2 Wires 40% (in.²)	1 Wire 53% (in.²)
⅜	—	—	—	—	—
½	0.660	0.342	0.106	0.137	0.181
¾	0.864	0.586	0.182	0.235	0.311
1	1.105	0.959	0.297	0.384	0.508
1¼	1.448	1.646	0.510	0.658	0.872
1½	1.683	2.223	0.689	0.889	1.178
2	2.150	3.629	1.125	1.452	1.923
2½	2.557	5.135	1.592	2.054	2.722
3	3.176	7.922	2.456	3.169	4.199
3½	3.671	10.584	3.281	4.234	5.610
4	4.166	13.631	4.226	5.452	7.224

Liquidtight Flexible Nonmetallic Conduit

Trade Size (in.)	Internal Diameter (in.)	Total Area 100% (in.²)	2 Wires 31% (in.²)	Over 2 Wires 40% (in.²)	1 Wire 53% (in.²)
⅜	0.494	0.192	0.059	0.077	0.102
½	0.632	0.314	0.097	0.125	0.166
¾	0.830	0.541	0.168	0.216	0.287
1	1.054	0.872	0.270	0.349	0.462
1¼	1.395	1.528	0.474	0.611	0.810
1½	1.588	1.979	0.614	0.792	1.049
2	2.033	3.245	1.006	1.298	1.720

Liquidtight Flexible Nonmetallic Conduit

Trade Size (in.)	Internal Diameter (in.)	Total Area 100% (in.²)	2 Wires 31% (in.²)	Over 2 Wires 40% (in.²)	1 Wire 53% (in.²)
⅜	0.495	0.192	0.060	0.077	0.102
½	0.630	0.312	0.097	0.125	0.165
¾	0.825	0.535	0.166	0.214	0.283
1	1.043	0.854	0.265	0.341	0.452
1¼	1.383	1.501	0.465	0.600	0.796
1½	1.603	2.017	0.625	0.807	1.069
2	2.063	3.341	1.036	1.336	1.771

Dimensions and Percent Area of Conduit and Tubing *(continued)*

Liquidtight Flexible Metal Conduit

Trade Size (in.)	Internal Diameter (in.)	Total Area 100% (in.²)	2 Wires 31% (in.²)	Over 2 Wires 40% (in.²)	1 Wire 53% (in.²)
⅜	0.494	0.192	0.059	0.077	0.102
½	0.632	0.314	0.097	0.125	0.166
¾	0.830	0.541	0.168	0.216	0.287
1	1.054	0.872	0.270	0.349	0.462
1¼	1.395	1.528	0.474	0.611	0.810
1½	1.588	1.979	0.614	0.792	1.049
2	2.033	3.245	1.006	1.298	1.720
2½	2.493	4.879	1.513	1.952	2.586
3	3.085	7.475	2.317	2.990	3.962
3½	3.520	9.731	3.017	3.893	5.158
4	4.020	12.692	3.935	5.077	6.727
5	—	—	—	—	—
6	—	—	—	—	—

Rigid Metal Conduit

Trade Size (in.)	Internal Diameter (in.)	Total Area 100% (in.²)	2 Wires 31% (in.²)	Over 2 Wires 40% (in.²)	1 Wire 53% (in.²)
⅜	—	—	—	—	—
½	0.632	0.314	0.097	0.125	0.166
¾	0.836	0.549	0.170	0.220	0.291
1	1.063	0.888	0.275	0.355	0.470
1¼	1.394	1.526	0.473	0.610	0.809
1½	1.624	2.071	0.642	0.829	1.098
2	2.083	3.408	1.056	1.363	1.806
2½	2.489	4.866	1.508	1.946	2.579
3	3.090	7.499	2.325	3.000	3.975
3½	3.570	10.010	3.103	4.004	5.305
4	4.050	12.883	3.994	5.153	6.828
5	5.073	20.213	6.266	8.085	10.713
6	6.093	29.158	9.039	11.63	15.454

Rigid PVC Conduit, Schedule 80

Trade Size (in.)	Internal Diameter (in.)	Total Area 100% (in.²)	2 Wires 31% (in.²)	Over 2 Wires 40% (in.²)	1 Wire 53% (in.²)
½	0.526	0.217	0.067	0.087	0.115
¾	0.722	0.409	0.127	0.164	0.217
1	0.936	0.688	0.213	0.275	0.365
1¼	1.255	1.237	0.383	0.495	0.656
1½	1.476	1.711	0.530	0.684	0.907
2	1.913	2.874	0.891	1.150	1.1523
2½	2.290	4.119	1.277	1.647	2.183
3	2.864	6.442	1.997	2.577	3.414
3½	3.326	8.688	2.693	3.475	4.605
4	3.786	11.258	3.490	4.503	5.967
5	4.768	17.855	5.535	7.142	9.463
6	5.709	25.598	7.935	10.239	13.567

Dimensions and Percent Area of Conduit and Tubing *(continued)*

Rigid PVC Conduit, Schedule 40, and HDPE Conduit

Trade Size (in.)	Internal Diameter (in.)	Total Area 100% (in.²)	2 Wires 31% (in.²)	Over 2 Wires 40% (in.²)	1 Wire 53% (in.²)
½	0.602	0.285	0.088	0.114	0.151
¾	0.804	0.508	0.157	0.203	0.269
1	1.029	0.832	0.258	0.333	0.441
1¼	1.360	1.453	0.450	0.581	0.770
1½	1.590	1.986	0.616	0.794	1.052
2	2.047	3.291	1.020	1.316	1.744
2½	2.445	4.695	1.455	1.878	2.488
3	3.042	7.268	2.253	2.907	3.852
3½	3.521	9.737	3.018	3.895	5.161
4	3.998	12.554	3.892	5.022	6.654
5	5.016	19.761	6.126	7.904	10.473
6	6.031	28.567	8.856	11.427	15.141

Type A, Rigid PVC Conduit

Trade Size (in.)	Internal Diameter (in.)	Total Area 100% (in.²)	2 Wires 31% (in.²)	Over 2 Wires 40% (in.²)	1 Wire 53% (in.²)
½	0.700	0.385	0.119	0.154	0.204
¾	0.910	0.650	0.202	0.260	0.345
1	1.175	1.084	0.336	0.434	0.575
1¼	1.500	1.767	0.548	0.707	0.937
1½	1.720	2.324	0.720	0.929	1.231
2	2.155	3.647	1.131	1.459	1.933
2½	2.635	5.453	1.690	2.181	2.890
3	3.230	8.194	2.540	3.278	4.343
3½	3.690	10.694	3.315	4.278	5.668
4	4.180	13.723	4.254	5.489	7.273
5	—	—	—	—	—
6	—	—	—	—	—

Type EB PVC Conduit

Trade Size (in.)	Internal Diameter (in.)	Total Area 100% (in.²)	2 Wires 31% (in.²)	Over 2 Wires 40% (in.²)	1 Wire 53% (in.²)
½	—	—	—	—	—
¾	—	—	—	—	—
1	—	—	—	—	—
1¼	—	—	—	—	—
1½	—	—	—	—	—
2	2.221	3.874	1.201	1.550	2.053
2½	—	—	—	—	—
3	3.330	8.709	2.700	3.484	4.616
3½	3.804	11.365	3.523	4.546	6.024
4	4.289	14.448	4.479	5.779	7.657
5	5.316	22.195	6.881	8.878	11.764
6	6.336	31.530	9.774	12.612	16.711

Dictionary
of Terms

A

Accessible: Easy to get to. An electrical outlet is said to be accessible if it can be worked on without disturbing the finish or construction of a house.

Accessible, readily: Can be reached quickly for operation, renewal, or inspection without climbing over or removing obstacles or using ladders, etc.

Alternating current: In alternating current, the voltage flows in one direction one instant, and the other direction the next instant. The direction of flow reverses continually. Each two reversals is called a cycle. The number of cycles per second is called frequency. In the United States, most systems are 60 cycles.

Ammeter: Instrument used to measure the amount of electric current.

Ampacity: Current-carrying capacity of conductor expressed in amperes.

Ampere: Unit of measure of the flow of electricity. Various parts of a wiring system — fuses, wall switches, fuse boxes, etc. — are rated in amperes. Ratings in amperes indicate the greatest amount of current with which these parts should be used.

Appliance, fixed: Appliance fastened or otherwise secured at specific location.

Appliance, portable: Appliance that can be easily moved from one place to another in normal use.

Appliance, stationary: An appliance that is not easily moved from one place to another in normal use.

Appliance branch circuit: Branch circuit for kitchen and dining areas, normally 20 amperes.

Approved: Signifies that minimum established standards have been met.

Arc, electric: Sustained visible discharge of electricity across gap in circuit or between electrodes. Arcing takes place in switches and other make-and-break devices when a circuit is opened, and at the brushes of a commutator-type motor if brush contact is bad.

Armored cable: A flexible, metallic sheathed cable used for interior wiring. Commonly called BX.

Askarel: A general term used for a group of nonflammable synthetic chlorinated hydrocarbons used as electrical insulating liquid.

Atom: Smallest particle that makes up an element. The element retains its characteristics when subdivided into atoms. Examples of elements are hydrogen, oxygen, and helium. Over 100 elements have been identified.

Attachment plug (cap): Device that makes an electrical connection between the conductors of the attached flexible cord and the electrical conductors in the receptacle.

Audible signal system: Signal system that depends on sense of hearing to attract attention.

Automatic: Self-acting. Operating by own mechanism when actuated by some influence.

B

Bare conductor: An electrical conductor having no insulation or covering of any sort.

Battery: Device that changes chemical energy into electrical energy.

Bonding: A permanent joining of metallic parts in circuitry that forms an electrical path. It ensures electrical continuity and is able to conduct safely any current likely to be imposed.

Bonding jumper: A reliable conductor that ensures the required bond or electrical continuity between metal parts that are required to be electrically connected.

Branch circuit: Circuit that supplies a number of outlets for lighting or appliances.

Building: A stand-alone structure that is cut off from adjoining structures by fire walls. All openings in the wall are protected by fire doors.

Burrs (conduit): Rough edges of metal that result when cutting conduit. These must be removed to prevent damage to wire insulation.

Bus bar: A heavy, solid conductor at the main power source to which branch circuits are connected.

BX: Term commonly used to identify armored cable.

C

Cabinet: A surface or flush-mounted enclosure that has a frame mat or trim to which a swinging door or doors can be hung.

Cable, electrical: Conductor that consists of two or more insulated wires grouped together in overall covering.

Candlepower: Term that expresses intensity of a beam of light.

Circuit: Path of electric current from a source (generator), through components (such as electric lights), back to the source.

Circuit breaker: Electromagnetic or thermal (heat operated) device that opens a circuit when the current in the circuit exceeds a predetermined amount. Circuit breakers can be reset.

Circuit breaker, adjustable: A circuit breaker that can be set to trip at various current values.

Clockwise: Moving in same direction as hands of a clock.

Closed circuit: Electrical circuit that provides path for the flow of current.

Coaxial cable: Power transmission line consisting of two conductors insulated from each other.

Code, National Electrical: Set of rules sponsored by National Fire Protection Association Purpose: To safeguard persons, buildings, contents, from hazards arising from use of electricity. Compliance will result in installations essentially free from hazard, but not necessarily efficient or adequate. The code is not intended as a manual of instruction for untrained persons. The National Electrical Code book, which is ordinarily revised every three years, is available from the:

National Fire Protection Association, Inc.
1 Batterymarch Park
Quincy, MA 02169.

Color coding: Identifying conductors by color to make sure the hot, or current-carrying, wires will be connected to hot wires, and the neutral wire will run in continuous circuits back to the ground terminals.

Common ground connection: Location where two or more continuous grounded wires terminate.

Concealed: Made inaccessible by the structure or finish of a building. Wires in concealed raceways are considered concealed even though they become accessible by pulling them out of the raceway.

Conductor: Material through which an electric current can flow easily. Copper wire, used in most house wiring, is a good conductor. Aluminum is also a good conductor, and is frequently used in transmission lines. Electrical energy is transferred by means of movement of free electrons that move from atom to atom inside conductor.

Conductor, bare: Conductor that has no covering or insulation.

Conductor, covered: A conductor covered with a material not recognized as insulation by the code.

Conductor, insulated: A conductor covered with material recognized by the code.

Conduit: Metal or fiber pipe or tube used to enclose electrical conductors.

Conduit body: Separate part of a conduit system that gives access through a removable cover.

Connector, solderless: Device that establishes connection between two or more conductors by means of mechanical pressure, without using solder.

Continuous duty: Designed to operate at a substantially constant load for a long, indefinite time.

Continuous load: A load where the maximum current is expected to last over three hours.

Controller: One or more devices that govern the electrical power delivered to the rotating machine or apparatus to which it is attached.

Convenience outlet: Electrical outlet that is part of a general lighting circuit. An outlet not intended for use of heavy equipment.

Counterclockwise: Moving in a direction opposite to the path followed by the hands of a clock.

Current-limiting overcurrent protective device: A device that, when interrupting currents in its limit range, will reduce the current flowing in the faulty circuit to a magnitude much less than that which the circuit could carry if the device were replaced with a solid conductor with the same impedance.

D

Device (electrical): Unit or component designed to carry but not to consume current. Examples—receptacle, switch.

Direct current: Current that flows in only one direction. Batteries (storage, dry cell) are important sources of direct current.

Disconnecting means: One or more devices or other means for disconnecting the conductors of a circuit from their electrical power source.

Dry cell: A nonspill type of cell that produces electricity by chemical action.

Dry location: An area that will not be exposed to moisture.

Dustproof: Constructed so dust will not interfere with its successful operation.

Dust tight: Constructed in such a way that dust cannot enter under specified test conditions.

Duty, continuous: Operation at a substantially constant load for an indefinitely long time.

Duty, intermittent: Operation for alternate intervals of (1) load and no load; or (2) load and rest; or (3) load, no load, and rest.

Duty, periodic: Intermittent operation in which the load conditions are regularly recurrent.

Duty, short-time: Operation at a substantially constant load for a short and definitely specified time.

Duty, varying: Operation at loads, and for intervals of time, both of which can be subject to wide variation.

Dwelling: One or more rooms for the use of one or more persons as a housekeeping unit with space for eating, living, sleeping, and permanent provisions for cooking and sanitation.

Dwelling, multifamily: A building containing three or more dwelling units.

Dwelling, one-family: A building consisting of one dwelling unit.

Dwelling, two-family: A building consisting of two dwelling units.

E

Electric current: Flow of electrons through a conductor. To determine the amount of electricity (number of electrons) flowing through the conductor, it is necessary to measure the current. The rate of electron flow is measurement in *amperes.* A unit quantity of electricity is moved through an electric circuit when one ampere of current flows for one second of time. This unit is called a *coulomb.*

Electric service panel: Main panel or cabinet through which electricity is brought into the building and distributed to branch circuits. Contains main disconnect switch for entire wiring system, also circuit breakers or fuses for individual circuits.

Electrolyte: Solution of a substance that is capable of conducting electricity. It can be in the form of a liquid or a paste.

Electromagnet: Magnet made by passing current through coil of wire wound on a soft iron core.

Enclosed: Covered by a case, housing, or walls that prevent accidental contact with energized parts.

Enclosure: Case or housing for apparatus or the fence around an installation to keep persons from accidentally touching energized parts. Also, to protect the equipment from physical damage.

Energize: To apply electrical voltage to or through.

Equipment: A general, all-inclusive term for material, fittings, devices, appliances, fixtures, apparatus, etc., used as a part of or in connection with an electrical installation.

Exposed (applied to house wiring): Designed for easy access.

F

Feeder: Circuit conductor between service equipment or generator switchboard and branch-circuit overcurrent device (fuse or circuit breaker).

Finger-tight: Tightened with the fingers.

Fish tape (wire): Flat spring steel wire used to fish (pull) wires through conduit or walls.

Fitting: Accessory such as a bushing, or locknut used on wiring system intended primarily to perform a mechanical rather than electrical function.

Flexible: Something that can be bent without breaking.

Flexible cable or cord: Conductor made of a number of strands of wire of small diameter.

Foot-candle: Measurement of light. Amount of illumination when one lumen (*see lumen*) falls on one square foot of surface.

Footlambert: Measurement of light. Brightness of a surface that emits or reflects one lumen (*see lumen*) per square foot of its surface.

Fuse: Safety device inserted in series with a circuit. Contains metal that will melt or break when current is increased beyond specific value for definite period of time.

G

Ground: Connection between electrical circuit or equipment and the earth (or to a body that serves in place of the earth).

Grounded: Connected to earth or to some conducting body that serves in place of the earth. In an electrical wiring system, the grounded wire is always white.

Grounding conductor: Wire, in circuit, (green) used as safety measure. During normal use of a circuit, the grounding wire is not in use. In an abnormal situation, (for example) when a live wire accidentally comes in contact with the frame of a washing machine, grounding wire grounds circuit to prevent fire and injury from electrical shock.

Grounding electrode conductor: The conductor that connects the grounding electrode to the equipment grounding conductor and/or the source of a separately derived system.

Ground fault circuit interrupter: A protective device that de-energizes a circuit or part of it within an established time period that is less than the time required to operate the overcurrent protective device of the circuit.

Guarded: Covered, shielded, fenced, enclosed, or protected in some way by covers, casings, barriers, rails, screens, mats, or platforms to remove the likelihood of persons or objects coming in contact.

H

Hazardous locations: Places where fire or explosion is possible due to flammable gases or vapors, flammable liquids, combustible dust, or ignitable fibers or flyings.

Horsepower: Unit of electrical energy equal to 746 watts of electrical power.

Hot wires: Wires that carry power (their insulation can be any color except white, gray, and green).

Hydrometer: Instrument used to measure specific gravity of a liquid (ratio of weight of battery electrolyte to same volume of water).

I

Identified: Possible to recognize as suitable for the specific purpose, function, use, environment, application, etc., where described in a particular code requirement.

Insulation: Noncurrent-carrying materials used on the outside of wires, and in the construction of electrical devices.

Insulator: Nonconductor used to support current-carrying conductor.

Isolated: Object that is not readily accessible without using special means for access.

J

Junction box: Box in which conductors (wires) are joined.

K

Kilo: Prefix meaning 1000.

Knockout: Circular metal die-cut impression in outlet and switch boxes, not completely severed, that can be removed to accommodate wiring.

L

Lead-acid battery: Active materials in a lead-acid storage battery are lead peroxide (used as positive cell) and sponge lead (used as negative plate). Electrolyte is a mixture of sulfuric acid and water.

Light, measuring: Light is measured in candlepower, lumens, foot-candles, and footlamberts.

Quantity	Unit
Intensity of light	Candlepower
Amount of light	Lumen
Level of light	Lumen
Level of illumination	Foot-candle
Brightness of surface	Foot-candle

Lighting outlet: Outlet intended for direct connection of lamp holder, lighting fixture, or pendant cord terminating in lamp holder.

Listed: Equipment or material included in a list published by an organization acceptable to the authority having jurisdiction and concerned with product evaluation. This organization maintains periodic inspection of production of the listed equipment or materials. Their listings also states either that the equipment or materials meet appropriate standards or has to be tested and found suitable for use in the specified manner.

Live parts: Electric conductors, buses, terminals, or components that are insulated or exposed and a shock hazard exists.

Load, continuous: Situation where maximum current is expected to continue for three hours or more.

Lumen: Light measurement that indicates amount of light cast upon one square foot of the inner surface of a hollow sphere of one foot radius with a light of one candle in its center.

M

Magnet: A substance that has the property of magnetism—the power to attract substances such as iron, steel, nickel. Magnets can be classified as temporary or permanent depending on their ability to retain magnetic strength after the magnetizing force has been removed.

Magnetize: Converting material into a magnet by rearrangement of molecules. Providing invisible force that causes material to attract steel.

Mechanically secure: A fastening that is rigid and so made that it will not come loose unless disturbed in unnatural manner.

Meter, construction: Small motor is connected so it turns when electricity is being used. When only a small amount of electricity is used, the motor turns slowly; when a large amount is used it turns rapidly. The motor turns gears that operate small numbered dials.

Meter, electric: Device that measures electricity used.

Milliammeter: An ammeter that measures current in thousandths of an ampere.

Molecule: Smallest particle to which a substance can be reduced and still be identified by the same name. Applies to all substances—solids, liquids, and gases.

N

National Electrical Code: *See Code, National Electrical.*

Nonconductors: Materials through which electric current does not flow. Typical examples are glass, porcelain, and rubber.

O

Ohm: Term used to indicate amount of electrical resistance in a circuit or electrical device. Resistance is often placed in a circuit to limit the amount of current that flows or to produce heat.

Ohmmeter: Instrument for directly measuring resistance in ohms.

Open circuit: Circuit that does not provide complete path for electric current to flow.

Outlet: Point of wiring system at which current is obtained to supply current consuming fixtures and equipment.

Overcurrent: Any current that exceeds the rated current of equipment or the ampacity of a conductor. Overcurrents can result in overloads, short-circuits, or ground faults.

Overcurrent protection: Fuse or circuit breaker used to prevent excessive flow or current.

Overload: Current demand that is greater than that for which circuit or equipment was designed.

P

Panelboard: A single panel or group of panel units that contain fuses and automatic overcurrent devices, with or without switches for the control of light, heat, or power circuits. They are designed to be contained inside cabinets or cutout boxes that are placed in or on a wall or partition. They are accessible only from the front.

Parallel connection: Electrical connection that provides more than one path for flow of electricity.

Polarizing: Identifying wires throughout the system by color to help ensure that hot wires will be connected only to hot wires and that neutral wires will run in continuous uninterrupted circuits back to the ground terminals.

Plug, attachment: Device that, by insertion in receptacle, establishes connection between conductors of attached flexible cord and conductors permanently connected to receptacle.

Polarity: A—Identification of voltage, negative or positive. B—Property of an electrical circuit to have positive and negative poles.

Power: Power, whether electrical or mechanical, pertains to rate at which work is being done. Work is done when a force causes motion. The basic unit of electrical power measurement is the watt.

Power outlet: An enclosed assembly that can include receptacles, circuit breakers, fuseholders, fused switches, fuses, and watt-hour meter mounting means. It is intended to supply and control electric power to mobile homes, RVs, and boats. Such an outlet can be used to supply power to temporarily installed equipment.

Premises wiring: Interior and exterior wiring including power, lighting, control, and signal circuit wiring together with all of its hardware, fittings, and devices that extend from the load end of the service drop, or load end of the service laterals, or source of a separately derived system to the outlet(s). Not included is internal wiring of appliances, fixtures, motors, controllers, motor control centers, and similar equipment.

Q

Qualified person: Person who is thoroughly familiar with construction and operation of apparatus and hazards involved.

R

Raceway: Channel that holds electrical conductors (wires, cables, and bars).

Rainproof: Constructed, protected, or treated so that rain cannot interfere with the successful operation of the apparatus under specified test conditions.

Receptacle: Contact device installed at an outlet for connection of a single attachment plug.

Receptacle outlet: Outlet where one or more receptacles are installed.

Rectifier: Device used to change alternating current to unidirectional (one direction) current.

Remote control circuit: Electrical circuit that controls another circuit through a relay or equivalent device.

Resistance, electrical: Quality of an electric circuit measured in ohms that resists the flow of current. All electrical conductors offer some resistance to flow of electric current. Conductors such as copper, silver, and aluminum offer but little resistance. Examples of poor conductors (insulators) are glass, wood, and paper.

Rheostat: Resistor that provides various amounts of resistance. Usually installed in series with load.

Romex: Nonmetallic sheathed cable used for indoor wiring.

Rotor: Portion of alternating current machine that turns or rotates.

S

Screw terminal: Means for connecting wiring to devices, which makes use of a threaded screw.

Series cable: Service conductors that have been made up in the form of a cable.

Series connection: Electrical connection where there is but a single path for electricity to flow.

Series wound: Motor or generator in which armature is wired in series with field winding.

Service conductors: Conductors that extend from street main or from a transformer to service equipment or premises being supplied with electrical service.

Service drop: Overhead service conductors from the last pole or other aerial support to (and including) the splices connecting to the service entrance conductors at the building or other structure.

Service equipment: Equipment located near the entrance of supply conductors that provide main control and means of cutoff (fuses or circuit breaker) for current supply to building.

Service lateral: Underground service conductors between the street main, including any risers at a pole or other structure or from transformers, and the first point of connection to the service entrance conductors in a terminal box or meter or other enclosure with adequate space, inside or outside the building wall. If there is no terminal box, meter, or other enclosure with adequate space, the point of connection is considered to be the point of entrance of the service conductors into the building.

Short circuit: Improper connection between hot wires, or between a hot wire and a neutral wire.

Skinning (wire): Removing insulation.

Solar voltaic system: All of the components and subsystems that, combined, convert solar energy into electrical energy suitable for connection to a load.

Solenoid: Electromagnetic coil that contains movable plunger.

Specific gravity: Ratio of the weight of a certain volume of liquid to the weight of same volume of water. Specific gravity of pure water is 1.000. Sulfuric acid used in storage batteries has a specific gravity of 1.830, thus sulfuric acid is 1.830 times as heavy as water. Specific gravity of a mixture of sulfuric acid and water can vary with the strength of the solution from 1.000 to 1.830. When a storage battery is discharged, the sulfuric is depleted and the electrolyte gradually changes into water. This action provides a guide in determining the state of discharge of a lead-acid battery. Specific gravity of battery electrolyte is measured with a hydrometer.

Specifications: Detailed descriptions that indicate manner of installation, standards of materials, quality of work, etc.

Splice: Connection made by connecting two or more wires.

Stator: Fixed portion of windings of ac machine.

Stranded wire or cable: Quantity of small conductor wires twisted or otherwise held together to form single conductor.

Switch, bypass isolation: A manually operated device used in conjunction with a transfer switch to provide a means of directly connecting load conductors to a power source, and of disconnecting the transfer switch.

Switch, general-use: A switch intended for use in general distribution and branch circuits. It is rated in amperes, and it is capable of interrupting its rated current at its rated voltage.

Switch, general-use snap: A form of general-use switch constructed so it can be installed in device boxes or on box covers, or otherwise used in conjunction with wiring systems recognized by the code.

Switch, isolating: A switch intended for isolating an electric circuit from the source of power. It has no interrupting rating, and it is intended to be operated only after the circuit has been opened by some other means.

Switch, motor-circuit: A switch, rated in horsepower, capable of interrupting the maximum operating overload current of a motor of the same horsepower rating as the switch at the rated voltage.

Switch, transfer: An automatic or nonautomatic device for transferring one or more load conductor connections from one power source to another.

Symbols (electrical): Arrangement of lines, letters, etc., used on plans to show where wiring circuits, switches, outlets, etc., are to be installed.

System (electrical): Electrical installation that is complete and will serve the purpose for which it is intended.

T

Tachometer: Instrument that indicates revolutions per minute.

Thermal cutout: Temperature controlled fuse that opens the circuit that powers a device when the temperature of that device rises to a high. Some thermal cutouts can be reset.

Three-way switch: Type of switch. Two 3-way switches are required to control a light from two different locations.

Torque: Turning effort or twist that a shaft provides when transmitting power.

Transformer: Device composed of two or more coils, linked only by magnetic lines of force, used to transfer energy from one circuit to another.

Transmission lines: Conductor or system of conductors used to carry electrical energy from source to load.

Tubing: Small pipe.

U

Underwriters label: Insurance companies, manufacturers, and other interested parties support testing labs under Underwriters' Laboratories. Manufacturers submit products to be tested for safety. Products that meet safety standards can use Underwriters label of approval when placed on the market.

V

Volt: Unit used to measure electrical pressure (corresponds to pounds of pressure in a water system).

Voltage: A measure of electrical pressure between two wires of electrical circuit.

Voltage drop: Loss of electrical current caused by overloading wires, or by using excessive spans of undersize wire. Two indications of voltage drop are dimming of lights and slowing down of motors.

Voltage to ground: For grounded circuits, this is the voltage between the given conductor and that point or conductor of the circuit that is grounded. For underground circuits, it is the greatest voltage between the given conductor and any other conductor of the circuit.

Voltmeter: Instrument used to measure the electrical pressure, or voltage, of a circuit.

W

Watt: Unit of measure of electric power. (Volts times amperes equals watts of electrical energy used.) One watt used for one hour is one watt hour; 1000 watt hours equal one kilowatt hour, unit by which electricity is metered and sold.

Wattmeter: Instrument used to measure electrical power in watts.

Wire: Electrical conductor in the form of a slender rod.

Wiring diagram (electrical): Drawing in the form of symbols that show conductors.

Answers to Review Questions

Unit 1
1. h.
2. b.
3. i.
4. d.
5. e.
6. f.
7. g
8. c.
9. a.

Unit 2
1. noncurrent.
2. larger.
3. 12, 14
4. black, white
5. black, white, red
6. True.
7. a. Nonmetallic sheathed cable.
   b. Flexible armored cable.
8. a. Lamp cords.
   b. Heater cords.
   c. Power or service cords.
9. d.
10. Underwriters' Laboratories

Unit 3
1. conduit
2. water pipe
3. connectors
4. oil, water
5. BX
6. in-wall.
7. number, size

Unit 4
1. True.
2. True.
3. True.
4. True.
5. a. Square.
   b. Octagon.
   c. Rectangular.
   d. Circular.
6. knockouts.
7. d.

Unit 5
1. two, one
2. three, two
3. four, three
4. mechanical parts
5. False.
6. 3-way.
7. a. Wall outlets.
   b. Fluorescent lights.
   c. Appliances.
   d. Motor-driven equipment.

Unit 6
1. c.
2. d.
3. a.
4. f.
5. e.
6. b.

Unit 7
A. Extension rule.
B. Auger bit.

C. Lineman's pliers.
D. Soldering gun.
E. Multipurpose tool.
F. Conduit bender.
G. Push-pull tape rule.
H. Stubb or close quarter
    screwdriver.
I. Keyhole saw.
J. Fish tape.
K. Curved jaw pliers.
L. Test light.

Unit 8

1. False.
2. True.
3. False.
4. False.
5. True.
6. False.
7 True.

Unit 9

1. 120, 240
2. two
3. True.
4. a. main switch.
   b. circuit breaker.
   c. fuse.
5. 100
6. amperage
7. kitchen, dining area, laundry
8. two
9. amperage rating

Unit 10

1. codes
2. covering
3. True.

4. shock
5. hacksaw, metal-cutting shears
6. Bushings
7. True.
8. hacksaw, threadless
9. False.
10. water pipe

Unit 11

1. color
2. False.
3. conductor
4. 240
5. brass, silver
6. False.
7. metal boxes
8. tap
9. d.
10. overloads, short
11. overload
12. proper

Unit 12

No questions.

Unit 13

1. False.
2. a. armored (BX) cable.
   b. plastic cable.
   c. nonmetallic sheathed cable.
3. hot, grounded, overloaded
4. Grounding type.
5. template
6. five
7. hot

Unit 14

No questions.

Index